Seasonal Structure for Crappie

by
Tim Huffman

Published by
Huffman Publishing
PO Box 26
Poplar Bluff, MO 63902

All rights reserved. Except for brief, appropriate excerpts for reviews, no parts of this book may be reproduced in any form without written permission from the publisher.

Printed in USA by: Corning Publishing Company
810 N. Missouri Ave.
Corning, AR 72422

Cover design by: Scott Wunder
Drawings by: Chris Grobe

copyright 1997
Printed Feb. 1998

This book is dedicated to my sons, Landon and Travis. They're avid sportsmen who love the outdoors. The many hours we've spent together in sports, hunting and fishing have been among the best of my life. They're not just sons, they're my friends. I look forward to many more good years with them.

At the time of this printing, Landon is stationed in Texas serving in the U.S. Air Force. Travis is a junior at Poplar Bluff, MO, high school.

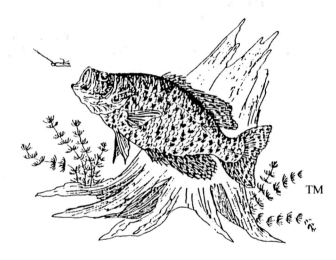

Huffman Publishing
Outdoor Education & Entertainment

Section 1 Channels Ledges, & Drop-Offs

CHAPTER 1   page 13
Deep Channel Ledges
    An easy-to-find structure offering crappie comfortable water temperatures during extreme heat and cold seasons.

CHAPTER 2   page 26
Mid Depth Ledges
    The best year-round seasonal structure.

CHAPTER 3   page 37
Shallow Water Ledges
    A 'hot' structure when conditions are right.

CHAPTER 4   page 45
Secondary Ledges
    Non-channel ledges offer an optional holding site for crappie to use.

CHAPTER 5   page 53
Creek/River Intersections
    Intersections are the highway crossroads of the underwater world.

Section 2 Man-Made Structures

CHAPTER 6   page 63
Concrete Bridge Pilings
    A popular, simple structure for crappie.

CHAPTER 7   page 73
Man-Made Rocky Banks
    Rip-rap, dikes, and wake walls provide a primary structure enjoyed by many species of fish and bait.

CHAPTER 8   page 81
Floating Docks
    A man-made structure providing shade and cover for fish.

Section 3 Wood Structures

CHAPTER 9   page 91
Man-Made Wood Structure
    Creating your own 'crappie hole' pays big dividends.

CHAPTER 10   page 103
Stumps, Snags, & Logs
    It's difficult to beat the real thing....natural wood.

TABLE OF CONTENTS

CHAPTER 11   page 113
Fallen Trees (Laydowns)
    A laydown in deep water offers everything a crappie could want.

Section 4 Natural Structures

CHAPTER 12   page 127
Points
    Each point is different, but most are runways for crappie to follow to reach their favorite depth for the conditions.

CHAPTER 13   page 135
Deep (& Mid Depth) Weeds
    Never-ending changes in deep weeds make them a challenge.

CHAPTER 14   page 141
Rock Bluffs
    Bluffs provide a wide range of depths with an ample supply of food.

CHAPTER 15   page 149
Shallow Flats
    When hot, there's no better place to fish.

CHAPTER 16   page 156
Mid Depth Flats
    An any-technique zone and structure; easy, relaxed fishing.

CHAPTER 17   page 161
Deep Flats
    An option for fish to use when in deep water.

CHAPTER 18   page 169
Humps
    Electronics and fisherman education have made humps a popular new target of many fishermen.

CHAPTER 19   page 175
High Water Structure
    How to fish when the rains cause a rise.

Introduction

Seasonal Structures

Seasonal Structure for Crappie is designed for one reason -- to help you catch more fish.
    I can assume that you're reading this for one of two reasons (or maybe both): to learn how to put a few more fish in the livewell on a consistent basis and for the enjoyment of reading about crappie fishing. There's nothing wrong with either.
    Why write this particular book? Because it parallels the popular column by the same name appearing in each issue of *Crappie* magazine. The article's success must mean that it's helping fishermen catch crappie and giving them a little more knowledge to go with their experience. Therefore, this book combines several structures in one volume that can be used as a reference guide for many years.
    Seasonal Structure is written in a slightly different format than the column to provide loyal readers with something different, yet it gives the same type information, illustrations and photos.

Seasonal Structure 8

Section 1
Channels, Ledges, & Drop-offs

-Ledges
    -Shallow
    -Middle Depths
    -Deep
    -Secondary
-Creek/ River Intersections

Seasonal Structure

General Information about:
Channels, Ledges & Drop-offs

A ledge is the overall number one structure element for catching crappie. A ledge has it all: deep water for safety from predators; different zones for varying light penetration; a comfort zone when the barometric pressure takes a quick rise or fall; an edge that is used for a reference when traveling or feeding; associated flats for feeding and normal movements; a food supply because all fish, including baitfish, reference to a ledge; and a natural cover that's present along most channels.

Deep water is important to fish. Therefore, a ledge, also called a drop-off, is the perfect spot for a crappie. A channel is the first thought when a ledge is mentioned. The channel provides deeper water on the lower portion of a drop-off. A channel may be a small creek or a huge river channel.

There are many ledges other than those found along channels. A steep bank is actually a ledge. The top of the ledge is above water with the drop-off region being partially in the water.

Secondary ledges are very common and an excellent place to find crappie. Although a secondary ledge may only have a drop of a foot, it does provide deeper water than surrounding bottom at and above the ledge top.

Another factor is light penetration. This is important. The results can be seen in fish activity. Early morning and late afternoon are good times to catch crappie. Why? Because the light penetration is low. They can see a bait and are actively feeding. As the sun rises, fish are likely to move deeper and sometimes turn off. You've probably seen this in your fishing many times.

Barometric pressure has a definite influence on crappie. A cold front is the most popular spring weather factor that plays havoc with fish catching. A barometric change will usually effect shallow fish the most, causing them to stay and not bite, or move a little deeper. Even fish in deeper water will be in a negative or neutral feeding mood. The pressure influence is bad.

One note about barometric pressure: the approach of a front is a good time to catch fish. They actively feed with the approach, continue to feed when it arrives, and shut down after it has passed.

When mentioning ledges as references for travel, it's common to compare them to a highway system. Without a compass and map, it would be difficult for you to travel from town to town. Just think: no roads, fences, or familiar landmarks; travel would make travel difficult or impossible. Just as roadways give us a logical travel path and reference, ledges give crappie highways to travel. Crossroads include creek inlets and other contour changes. Fish don't have to use a drop, but it has been proven to be a favorite structure for them.

Feeding is no problem on a ledge. Forage likes to stay in comfort zones, too. They also follow logical travel paths (although not as much as game fish). Flats next to ledges, cover, and the drop-off itself are places for crappie to feed.

Cover along a ledge can be natural or man-made (placed by fishermen). Natural cover, primarily stumps, are often present. Crappie draw to these structures like metal shavings to a magnet. Wood is a security blanket that gives protection from predators, blocks current, and gives an ambush spot for feeding.

Chapter 1

Deep Channel Ledges

The top of a deep ledge is 15-30 feet in a typical stained lake. Deep, clear lakes will be 25-50 feet deep while shallow lakes may have deep drops as shallow as 10 feet.

Where? Deep ledges are found in any moderately deep lake, reservoir or river. The only waters where they are not found is very shallow lakes, most ponds and a few of the bowl shaped lakes.

Deep ledges are excellent deep water hangouts for crappie. The zone often has good water temperatures even during extreme heat and cold conditions. Fishing a ledge is the best way to find numbers of deep crappie.

Locating is accomplished with a locator and topo map. First, look at the map and mark some deep ledges. Suppose you select a 20 foot ledge on the map. When on the water, align points, inlets or other structures to follow in finding the ledge. If you line up two points, you simply motor from one point toward the other until your locator shows the drop.

Things change when a map is not available. Hopefully, you have had some experience on the lake so you'll know the approximate locations of drop-offs. If not, visually select two objects on opposite banks. Slowly motor from one side to the other. A ledge or channel will quickly show on your locator.

WINTER
Rating: 10

Winter is an excellent season for deep ledge crappie. Winter is a time when fish need proper water conditions. Main river channels are often the prime target to get the best water. The deepest water, even if it isn't used, is often a drawing card for crappie. The best thing about primary channels is they're easy to find and fish.

Specific items to look for are bends, cuts, irregular features and cover. The combination of wood and a good ledge can gather hundreds of crappie into a spot the size of a boat. I don't know why they group so tightly in the winter, but it makes catching fast and furious when one of these spots are found.

Winter fishing from a boat allows several different methods. Two techniques are particularly suited for winter. Very slow, vertical trolling and anchor casting are excellent for creeping a bait along good locations.

Slow vertical presentations require boat control. Once fish are found, the boat must remain in place without spooking the fish. Deep water reduces spooking, but care should still be taken.

It's wise to mark a spot immediately when a fish is caught. A buoy can be thrown or you can align objects on the bank. Either way, note your position above water and on the locator for underwater depth and cover.

15   Deep Channel Ledge

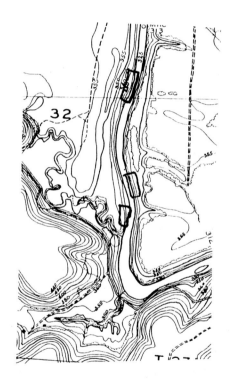

Deep Drop-Offs
The circled examples range from 10-20 feet on top down to 35-45 feet. On clear, deep lakes, a deep drop may start at 30 to 40 feet.

Anchoring is the best technique for catching fish from a small area such as a group of stumps. Anchoring lets a fisherman repeat casting to a specific spot. An area can be thoroughly worked before moving.

Another advantage is boat control. There are no worries about keeping the boat in a certain spot, position, etc. If you anchor, you can put your back to the wind and enjoy fishing.

A disadvantage of anchoring is that a fisherman needs to know where the fish are likely to be and anchor accordingly. It's not a good method for randomly searching for fish.

S-l-o-w is the word for deep, winter crappie. Fish will often hit solid, but they want the bait still or barely moving. (I know, you're reading this thinking about the times when you pulled a bait at a fairly rapid speed and tore-up the December and January crappie. There are exceptions to every rule because of weather conditions, water conditions and individual lake characteristics. Slow is the rule-of-thumb and should be the starting place for working a bait).

Minnows are a top winter bait because of slow presentations. When presented slow, a minnow offers the perfect action of a real minnow and the correct smell....it don't get no better. A minnow can be vertically fished over the side of a boat or away from the boat with a slip float. Either way, the bait can be left for a long period of time right in front of a crappie's nose. Minnows are great.

Jigs also work good and are the only choice for casting and dragging along the bottom. Twenty feet of water is deep, but a jig can be casted past the drop, settle down to the bottom and worked back slowly. It's a deadly presentation.

Deep Channel Ledge

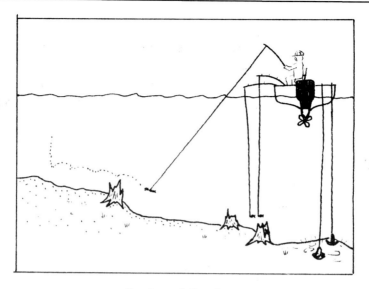

Anchored Casting

This technique is great for fishing open-water structures, including a deep ledge.

As shown here, anchors are dropped in a position to allow both tightlined poles and a jig being cast to be in potentially good areas. The two 'dead' poles tightlined over the side provide bonus baits (minnows) requiring little attention.

The jig can be used to reach and probe other cover.

It gives a one-two punch that can be effective.

Seasonal Structure 18

The best Jig? Typical jigs that have movement without being pulled. For example, a marabou is a top pick. The tube or tube/hair combinations are good. Just select your favorite jig that has some action with little or no movement and give it a try. Be sure to switch colors when action is slow.

The action upon retrieve should either be a continuous pull or a hop-pause-hop. The steady pull keeps a fisherman in constant contact with the jig. Every limb, rock or hit can be felt.

A hop-pause-hop has a magic appeal during certain time periods. A cast would go something like this: (1) Cast from deep water to shallow. (2) Let the jig settle to the bottom. Pop the rod tip up six to ten inches. (3) Drop the rod tip and count "One thousand one, one thousand two," and pop the tip again. Bites usually occur on the drop and the fish is hooked when the rod tip is popped.

Winter is the time for big fish, especially along a deep channel. Keep line, hook points and knots in top shape. Expect to catch a big one. Keep your net handy!

SUMMER
Rating: 9

Summer is another excellent season for deep ledge crappie. Although similar in desires and needs, crappie act differently in the summer than in the winter. They are less predictable and catching big ones can be difficult.

A fisherman can take his pick of methods for deep water. Obviously, some methods work better than others, but almost any presentation that gets to the fish has a legitimate chance to entice a strike.

The most catchable fish are those on or near bottom. Vertical presentations put baits down to the fish and baits stay in the strike zone. Therefore, vertical presentations are probably the most logical.

Another tactic that's very effective for summer fish is pulling. Pulling has been refined and made popular by super Pickwick guide, Roger Gant. Roger positions his boat sideways with his trolling motor positioned on the opposite side of his boat near the middle-front. He lets the wind push his boat and uses the trolling motor to position and control the pull.

Poles for pulling can be any type, but baitcasters with a seven foot rod is recommended. The baitcaster lets the jig fall while being pulled until it reaches the bottom and starts bumping. Two or three cranks gets it off the bottom and in perfect position for a bite. The long flexible rods make detecting strikes easy and are good leverage/shock absorption for hooking and fighting.

Pulling uses two theories: (1) most actively feeding fish are near the bottom and (2) baits need to be very visible because they come and go quickly when pulling. Heavier 1/8 ounce jigs

Roger Gant uses his pulling method to float sideways with the wind while using his trolling motor to keep him at a specific depth.

are the best choice for getting deep. Using two jigs per line really gets them down and keeps them there.

Vertical presentations are a little different. Jigs of all types will take summer crappie. However, this is the season when I definitely recommend minnows. There is a time frame in the summer when minnows will dramatically out-catch- jigs. Again, I'm not sure why this seasonal phase takes place, but fishermen across the south have proven this phenomenon over and over.

Presentations of the basic slow and steady retrieve seems to work fine. Others work, too. For example, it's comend of a pass, the boat is turned around. One or two poles catch a fish. The baits had gained speed and rose up in the water. The change triggered strikes.

To reproduce the above, boat speeds are increased and baits placed at different depths including some higher. A straight, faster speed doesn't always catch fish. Why? (If I knew all the answers I would be a national tournament champ). The fact is that changing speeds, moving baits up and down, and other irregularities often trigger summer fish.

One characteristic of water that must be considered is the thermocline. This is a horizontal depth where O_2 & pH are not suitable for fish..Yes, most fish can live below the thermocline for periods of time but their bodies will be in terrible conditions. The conditions hard on their bodies; the fish won't bite. The best place to fish is just above the thermocline.

Two questions you must ask: How do I find the depth of the thermocline and what does that do to deep crappie? The first answer comes from lowering minnows on hooks to different depths. The depth where minnows die is the thermocline. Another way is to use a Combo-C-Lector. This unit will give temperature and pH changes associated with a cline.

What does a crappie on an 18 foot ledge do when the thermocline is 12 feet? The fish will likely suspend directly over the ledge. Also, suspending positions usually have wood cover present. Do you remember seeing fish on the locator scattered or grouped in water above the bottom and away from or over cover? These suspended crappie are still relating to but are not against structure. They relate by suspending above it.

You've probably learned that most of the suspended fish are usually negative or neutral. It's still a good idea to try

FALL
Rating: 5

Fall crappie are active and feeding. There's plenty for fishermen to catch but they may be places other than deep ledges. The best time for a deep fall ledge is during a bad front or high water, but there will always be a few fish at any time.

Vertical presentations with any typical bait is a good way to start. Artificials should have plenty of action. Presentations should be varied to give crappie a chance to show which speed they prefer.

SPRING
Rating: 5

Spring is a time of hot and heavy action all over the lake. The deep ledges are good in early spring and are particularly good when a major cold front moves through.

I sound like a broken record when it comes to discussing deep ledges, but vertical is one of the best ways to get a bait into the deep zone and keep it there. Your favorite baits should be used here. A fisherman should be aware that changing types and colors may trigger more or fewer bites and therefore he should be changing baits frequently when there's no action.

Presentations should be varied to provide the most slow and methodical movements. Trying a variety of speeds is important, though, just to see what the fish will hit best.

FACTORS
Deep Drop-Offs

***Wind** -not a factor unless boat control is a problem.
***Cold Front** -deep fish less bothered than shallow fish.
***Clouds/Rain** -doesn't hurt unless fish start to roam.
***Sun** -improves deep drops.
***Mud** -ok, but fish may move shallow.
***Clear** -good for deep drops.
***Fast Rise/Fall** -fish may go shallow, but not always; fall is ok.
***Current** -poor condition for fishing deep.
***High Water** -will probably slow a deep ledge, but conditions will determine good or bad.
***Fishing Pressure** -locators have made deep ledges available to all fishermen; small waters get heavy pressure on deep ledges.

Chapter 2

Mid Depth Ledges

The top of a mid depth ledge is 8 to 15 feet in a typical, stained, reasonably deep lake. Deep, clear water lakes may be 12 to 25 feet while shallow lakes have 5-10 feet for their middle depths.

Most waters, especially manmade lakes, have middle depth drop-offs and ledges. Channels with mid depth ledges are normally in creeks, the upper river portion of a lake, or are associated with other seasonal structures like points, humps, depressions, etc. Ledges formed by creek channels will be the main topic of discussion in this section while specifics on points and other structures will be described later.

Why fish a middle depth zone? Because it is the 'best' seasonal structure available for year-round fishing. It's dynamite! Fish use it when migrating, feeding, and hiding from predators. The temperature comfort zone is great for all except extreme temperatures.

Similar to deep channel drop-offs, mid depth locations are found with a map and locator. The next best method is with a locator only.

SPRING
Rating: 10

The middle depths are the easiest to fish and a ledge is the best structure in open water; it's a deadly combination.

Target creek channels. Look for typical irregularities with associated wook cover. Look for typical irregularities with associated wood cover. Crappie may be stable or on the move, so don't stay too long in one place when there's no action.

Tactics and methods vary greatly from one fisherman to another and from lake to lake. Trolling is probably the most productive method for catching large numbers of fish under a wide range of conditions.

Slow vertical trolling is good at these depths. The most important feature of this tactic in the spring is that a fisherman can keep moving to find fish. When fish are found, he can stop and work the specific cover until the action stops.

Fast trolling is probably the most productive search method. This technique puts a number of baits in front of more fish than any other technique. Fast trolling is a fun way to search for fish, catch fish, watch the bottom contours, find cover, and relax.

Fast trolling is aggressive. Its basics include going forward in a boat with one or more rods out each side. Where legal, it's common to have three poles per fisherman out each side of the boat. The rod numbers simply puts more baits in the water to improve the odds of getting a bite. More baits means more bait colors and sizes while allowing different depths to be fished.

Line length for fast trolling is normally 30 to 60 feet. The boat speed and jig weight determines the depth of the baits. Line angle should be horizontal about 30 degrees from the top of the water. Watching line angle lets a fisherman maintain consistent depths.

Mid Deep Ledges

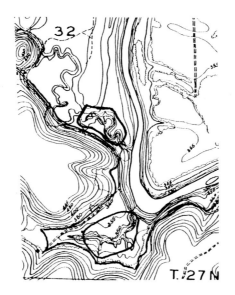

Mid Depth Drop-Offs
The middle depths provide some of the best fishing on a lake. Marked on the map are two creek channels that provide depths ranging from 5-15 feet on top down to 15-25.

Spring fast trolling means lots of action. There's always a percentage of fish holding on the mid depth ledges during the pre-spawn, spawn, and post-spawn.

Casting is a good tactic. The time for casting into open water is when specific targets have been located. For example, a stump or brush in 10 feet of water is a great target for casting.

Presentations can vary in the spring. Baits can be slow, medium, or fast speeds. Movements on the baits can vary, too. Try different things in the spring. Don't get in a rut by offering one bait at the same speed and action. Casting is a fun method of fishing that shouldn't be overlooked.

Last, but not least, vertical jigging a single log or stump. This isolates the game to one-on-one between you and the fish. Your presentation speed, action, and bait choice will determine the outcome. Baits like the McKala Reel Jig, Cabela's Maribou jig, Grizzly Google Eye feather jig are excellent for giving 'something different'.

Grizzly Google-Eye jig & McKala Reel Jig

SUMMER
Rating: 8

Summer can be a struggle for many fishermen. Fish often go to the shade of docks or floating vegetation, suspend over deep channels, and even go to the banks around wood cover. The mid depths are a place where fish can get above the thermocline while keeping a ledge and cover beside them.

Fast trolling is a top tactic because it eliminates wasted time trying to get negative fish, especially those suspending, to bite. It goes after crappie that are willing to take a bait as it passes by. This "take it now or forget it' theory is sometimes good for the summer fish.

Casting is another fun way to fish when crappie are cooperative. A creek ledge that swings near a shaded bank is a perfect spot to find aggressive crappie.

Slow trolling, slip-floating minnows and vertical jigging are other methods.

Baits. Most methods allow a fisherman to use his favorite bait. You should use a confidence bait except when there are limiting factors for using the bait. Speed and toughness eliminate some baits. For example, casting and fast trolling limits the baits used to artificials. (It's true that you can cast a minnow or a 1/64 ounce jig to objects away from the boat in 12 feet of water. However, it's not practical or wise when other baits do a much better job.)

Baits for casting include a regular tube jig, curly tail jig and just about anything else in the right size range you want to throw. Baits need to have a lot of action. Summer crappie can handle slightly faster speeds and will see the baits better if they have more movement. A 1/16 ounce is a good all-around

Tactics vary with technique and type of area fished. For example, there are two systems to use when casting an area. First, work a ledge that's 40 to 60 yards long. Cast to a different spot each time. This will present baits to fish scattered along the stretch. It also lets you learn the best spots and locate cover. The boat is less likely to spook the fish if it moves out of a spot periodically.

Tactic two is to pinpoint a certain area and keep casting to it until all the active fish are caught. This can be done from an anchored boat. When wanting to catch all fish possible from one spot, it's wise to change bait colors before moving to the next location. This will often trigger a few more bites.

Fast trolling tactics are different. Jig weights of 1/32 oz. are used to catch fish in shallow to mid depths. 1/16 oz. are used for fishing mid depths at a slow to medium trolling speed. Jig weights should vary to match the desired depth and boat speed.

Jigs with action should be your first pick for the techniques described here. Another bait popular with the pros is a plastic body with a feather or hair tail. The Hal-Fly is one example.

Fast trolling can also be done with small crankbaits. This tactic catches many species but will definitely put some good crappie in the boat. The best baits include Lewis Tiny Trap, Storm Pee Wee Wart, and other small crankbaits. The positive side to these baits is that they can catch big fish while the negatives include hangups and the loss of expensive baits.

FALL
Rating: 6

Crappie are on the move back and forth from deep to shallow water during the fall. Those mid depth crappie along ledges can sometimes be an easy catch...but not always. It's time to hit-and-run. Check as many spots as possible until fish are found. Don't waste time.

Fishing open water ledges in the fall is very enjoyable. Winds are normally mild. This is a big advantage over the same areas in the spring. Leaves are changing colors making everything bright and beautiful. The mornings are cool and the days mild. It's about as close to heaven as can get here on earth.

Fan-casting is good for quickly finding fish. Since fall crappie are not tight until the water really cools down, casting lets you catch the active fish and move on. However, fan-casting should not only cover an area, but it should also cover all depths.

A free-fall jig is another tactic to use. A countdown method is the best way to control depth. For example, the first cast can be counted down. "One thousand one, one thousand two, ..., one thousand six." This puts the bait at approximately six feet. The countdown is followed by a steady retrieve speed back to the boat. The next cast is a countdown to nine. Counts should be increased by two or three until a fish is caught or the jig hits bottom. Continue this process until a magic depth zone is found.

Trolling, pulling and vertical jigging are other techniques to successfully take fall crappie.

Jigs are used for casting, trolling and pulling. Vertical jigging can use either. The technique, temperatures, baitfish and fish size determines the size and type of baits. For example,

Seasonal Structure 32

Ledges produce many crappie throughout all seasons. Darrell Van Vactor displays a nice drop-off crappie taken from the northern area of Kentucky Lake.

what size are the shad? A very large minnow or jig may work better than a standard size. Are fish aggressive? A bait with action may out-fish a subtle jig. Are lake conditions terrible? A smaller jig with little movement is the best pick. Judgment should be used in selecting a bait that will catch fish under these conditions, knowing that changes should be made if needed.

Fall ledges are likely to have fish right on the break, along the top, and off to the side. Presentations should be made to these areas where the baits will be seen by the most fish.

Fishing a ledge requires requires you to pay attention. Know the depth of a bite, the speed of the bait, the action and angle of presentation. Also, be aware of the fish in relationship to the ledge. Was cover present where the fish was caught? Fish are usually doing the same thing all over a body of water where water conditions are similar. Pay attention, learn their pattern and catch fish in similar places to the one just fished.

WINTER
Rating: 6

Late fall and early winter is dynamite in the middle depth range along drop-offs. It's possibly the best weather, water and fish quality of the year. Action is excellent, the surroundings are beautiful, and mornings are very cool with perfect daytime temperatures. The number of sportsmen on the lake is down because of hunting. There are no jet ski's and pleasure boaters on the water.

Late fall and early winter crappie school. (Biologists say that it's not proper to call congregations of crappie 'schools'. However, to me it's a herd of cattle, covey of quail and a school of crappie). The fish are actively feeding, too. They are getting big and healthy.

In middle to late winter, the crappie move down to the bottom of the middle depth range and then on down to deeper water. This progression is natural with the time periods directly related to water temperature.

Anchored casting is an excellent method when crappie are schooled into tight groups. This not only lets casts be repeated to an active spot, but also relieves fishermen of the problem of boat control. Last but not least, an angler can put his back to a brisk northern wind and stay warmer than in a mobile boat.

A slip-float rig from an anchored boat is good for winter crappie. The depth can be quickly changed to put a bait at any depth and keep it there.

Practically any method that gets baits into the middle depths will work for winter crappie.

Presentations. The anchoring technique is one of the best ways to cast to a specific object or spot. Jigs let a fisherman work any depth in the middle zone. Casts are made while paying attention to wind and current. If a fish is caught at a certain depth and location, repeated casts are made. This gives you maximum control of a bait. Depth, speed and action is in your full control.

Casting jigs in the winter should be more subtle than the fast-action jigs of spring and summer. Tube jigs are the most commonly used crappie artificials. Winter is a perfect time for them. They have tail action to give the impression of life, but they don't have a big sway or ripple action like many jigs.

Jigs should be worked along and through cover on the drop-offs. Bouncing a jig on bottom may be the best presentation for triggering strikes. A lot of jigs will be lost, but the bottom can be felt, limbs and stumps found and fish caught.

Middepth Channel Ledge

Bob Holmes slow-trolling (spider rigging) a ledge at Pickwick Lake.

A 1/16 ounce jig is a perfect weight for depths of 8 to 15 feet. A slip-float and minnow can be deadly during the late fall and winter. A slip-float lets you cast long distances while keeping total control of the depth. When fishing from an anchored boat, two or three slip-float rigs can be scattered around near cover.

One tactic that has worked for me is to use one or two slip-float minnow rigs and one casting outfit. The slip-float rigs can be casted to potential areas and left alone. A free-fall jig can be casted to different areas. The floats can be watched for bites while the jig is retrieved. Any hits on the jig will be felt. This is a good one-two punch for mid depth crappie on a ledge.

FACTORS
Middle Depth Drop-Offs

* **Strong Frontal Passage** -can cause fish to become negative.
* **Clouds/Rain** -fish may go shallower.
* **Sun** -will drive shallow fish to the mid depths, but may drive some mid depth fish to deeper water.
* **Clear Water** -fish can become spooky with a boat over them.
* **Fast Rise/ Fall** -excellent depth to hold fish in changing conditions.
* **Current** -strong current is bad.
* **High Water** -ok in summer and winter, but bad in spring and fall.
* **Fishing Pressure** -depends upon the lake size, season and number of fishermen.

Chapter 3

Shallow Water Ledges

Shallow water means 3 to 8 feet at the top of a ledge. A clear lake will be deeper; muddy shallower at 3 to 5 feet.

A shallow ledge can be found in most lakes. Although shallow areas have less current and are often subject to silting, some areas in a lake are likely to have coves with old creek beds or other areas with drops. Shallow is relative, because at Reelfoot Lake a drop with a 4 foot ledge top that drops one foot down to 5 feet is an excellent place to look for crappie.

Shallow ledges are similar to their deeper counterparts. They are a reference for fish. Extreme temperatures are a hindrance to shallow ledges, but they have their place and time in the fishing seasons.

A deep drop can start at 20 feet and may drop down to 30. That's a change of 10 feet. A shallow drop may have the same change (10 feet) if the same channel swings into shallow water. However, the top of the ledge will start at 5 feet instead of 20.

Finding a shallow drop-off will simply be a matter of searching with a locator. A contour map may show these close contour lines next to shallow water, making it easy to start a search. Spending time on the water, looking for good spots, is the best method.

Seasonal Structure 38

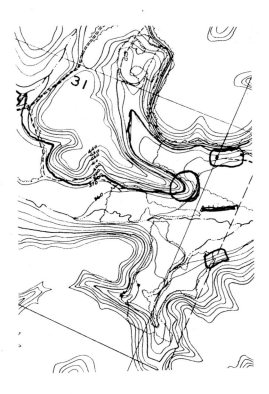

Shallow Water Drop-Offs

A locator is handy when looking for shallow drops. Since much of the shallow areas are sloping (not a sharp drop), the spot must be viewed with electronics to see what's below. These potential drops are next to the bank, but the best ones are likely to be in open water. Look for these along shallow, long points and flats.

SPRING
Rating: 10

This is the season to search the ledges associated with shallow water. It's no secret that the pre-spawn and spawn bring plenty of fish toward the banks to do their annual duty.

Specific areas to search include rocky shorelines where spawning is likely to take place. Main water areas are fine, but ledges in coves and creeks are much more likely to produce fish.

Casting is the best shallow tactic in the spring. It keeps a fisherman active and paying attention. A distance can be maintained to avoid spooking the fish. There's nothing like spring weather, casting and catching a few fish to shake the winter blues out of your body.

Casting can be done with a free-fall jig or a jig and float. The free-fall jig can be casted and let sink to any depth. The retrieve is worked in many different actions and speeds to fit the needs of the depths, cover and fish preference. Recommended jig: tube or curly tail on a 1/16 ounce head.

A float is an excellent way to control depth and work a jig very slow or at faster speeds. The float is an indicator for bites and should be sensitive to a bite. A 3/4 or 1 inch weighted styrofoam float, a small styrofoam float with a plastic stick, or a small plastic float will work properly. The heavier floats are easier to cast, but all three will do a good job. Jigs may be any weight (1/32, 1/16, 1/8) hair or tube jig.

Presentations of a free-fall jig should have a purpose whether made from an anchored or trolling motor controlled boat. The jig should first be a search weapon looking for the bottom contour and any cover that's present. Next, the jig should trigger any crappie in the area into a bite. Last and most importantly, it should be repeatedly cast into any potential area until there are no more bites.

The same presentations can be made from an anchored boat. Anchored fishing is less mobile so it should be done in an area where fish are known to be. This may be through experience and/or by watching a locator.

FALL
Rating: 7

Fall ledge characteristics are very similar to spring. Fish will actively feed and roam during this period.

Techniques are the same as in the spring.

Baits and presentations are the same as spring. The only difference is fall crappie are probably scattered more than in spring. As soon as the action becomes slow, move on.

Fall baits can be almost any type and action. Jigs with a slow fall (no heavier than 1/16) should be used in shallow areas.

SUMMER
Rating: 5

Early summer is a great time to take the family on a fishing trip. A good drop-off with a ledge top of 5 or 6 feet is perfect for inexperienced anglers to work a jig. Mix in a shore lunch and a little play time to complete the activities.

The key is to find a ledge that is being used by summer crappie. Depending upon the lake, it may not be an easy task. Look for areas that may be out of the main stream of traffic. For example, a channel in the back of a cove or a creek that swings in toward the bank. Finding fish may take a lot of scouting but once found will often be good every year.

With crappie on top of a ledge, casting a minnow and float is the easiest method. Fishermen of any skill level can fish

Summer baits in shallow water include a tube jig, curly tail, a minnow imitation like the AWD Firetail Delight, Road Runner, and Blue Fox Crappie Spin. Work the baits along and off of the ledge. Work spinner baits slightly faster to keep them off the bottom. Other baits can be presented with different speeds and actions.

WINTER
Rating: 3

Winter gets a low rating because crappie are seldom at these depths. However, when conditions are right with warming and sunshine, shallow ledges can be excellent spots.

The best shallow ledges are those close to large, very shallow flats. Flats warm quickly with southern breezes and sunshine, fish will move onto these flats and back down to deeper water. The transition position is the ledge. They travel up and over the ledge, often holding in that position until conditions are just right.

Casting a jig and float is the best technique. Depth is controlled with precision.

Jig size should be 1.5 to 2 inches long. Weight isn't critical provided it's matched with the float. Heavier jigs are an advantage for casting but may have quicker actions than a smaller jig.

Other top jigs for working under a float is a hair/feather jig, tube, and minnow tube. The marabou jig has a lot of action even with little movement. A bucktail has body yet very little movement. An in-between action jig is the plastic tube. All of these have characteristics that crappie favor depending upon their mood.

Winter means very slow to no speed at all. The float should be worked occasionally to give the bait action, but then

Seasonal Structure 42

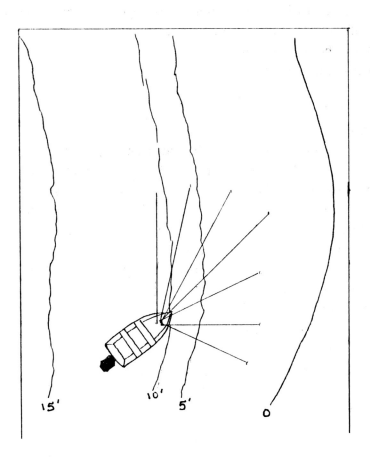

Fan-Casting

This method is excellent for quickly finding fish. Once an area has been checked and no fish caught, it's time to move on to another place. Once the crappie are found, action will be fast and wild.

set for two to seven seconds. This technique is dynamite when there is a small ripple on the water so the jig can be floated into the most active 'hot spot' with the ripples adding action to the bait by bouncing the float.

FACTORS
Shallow Water Channel Ledges

***Wind** -can cause mud if ledge is close to shore; can cool or warm water quickly.
***Cold Front** -bad; fish will probably move deeper or will stay and not bite.
***Clouds/Rain** -fish may scatter but are likely to follow the shallow ledges.
***Sun** -can totally shutoff fish or send them deep.
***Mud** -ok for warming in early spring, but bad most of the time.
***Clear** -must keep distance to avoid spooking fish.
***Fast Rise/Fall** -rise ok; fall will move fish deep.
***Current** -mild current ok.

Chapter 4

Secondary Ledges

The top of a secondary ledge is often 4 to 12 feet in stained water reservoirs. Shallow lakes will have deeper ledges; shallow lakes may have 2 to 8 feet deep ledges.

Lakes with a primary creek or river channel may have a ledge or ledges not associated with a channel. These shallower ledges usually have a drop from 1 to 4 feet. They are known as secondary drop-offs and are excellent locations for crappie.

Why fish? Secondary drops are good crappie structures. Many times fish will select a small drop over a large one. A secondary ledge is an excellent spot with the seasonal success being largely related to its depth.

Finding secondary ledges can be difficult. Many are found by accident while fishing. Others are found by studying a topo map and using a locator. Once found, make a menal note and mark the spot on your map.

Seasonal Structure 46

SPRING
Rating: 10

Locating ledges is a high priority when searching for crappie. A ledge may be under a dock, under a fallen tree, along a tree line or combined with a number of other structures. Although other structures are discussed separately, mixing a ledge with another structure is dynamite.

Spring is important to crappie fishing. Fish go into their baby-making mode to restock the population while fishermen get out to enjoy the fresh air and land some big slabs. Keeping these thoughts in mind, the obvious place to do both is on a shallow ledge. (If the ledge itself isn't suited for spawning, it will likely be a holding area for fish headed to and from the bank).

Note that a secondary dodge may only drop a foot or two. It doesn't take much to form a reference for crappie to use. This makes locating a subtle, secondary ledge a difficult chore, but finding one can be a gold mine.

Tip: The best secondary ledges in the spring will be near spawning banks.

The method for fishing a secondary ledge is determined by personal preference, depth of the ledge and associated cover. For example, if you like to slow troll, a secondary ledge is a good place for this method. You can gradually poke along the drop, keeping baits in the strike zone. You can spend some extra time on a stump or brush pile when one is found.

Casting, slip-floats, fast trolling and vertical jigging are all good methods. Again, depth is the major factor to determine which techniques will be the best. Once depth is known, select the method that will fit the cover. Open water allows trolling and casting. Stumps and brush piles are best fished with vertical techniques.

You can catch crappie in the spring with any bait presentation. Minnows are great for vertical presentations where slow, deliberate spots are fished. A minnow has natural action, visual and smell attractants.

Faster presentations let you choose your favorite artificial baits. The tube and curly tail are good standbys. A bait that's been around a long time but continues to be improved by many companies is the minnow imitation. Whether hollow or solid, the minnow imitations try to mimic the real thing while providing a tough, long-lasting bait that doesn't have to be babied in a minnow bucket. If you believe the 'big bait, big fish' theory, minnows are a perfect choice.

With the standard baits just mentioned, you can fish fast, slow or anywhere in-between. A popular tactic is to cast on top of a ledge and pull toward deeper water. The advantage is that the jig falls, but the continuously deeper water allows for the drop. A bait can be bumped along the bottom or worked over the top of the ledge and cover.

Shallow ledges in 5 or 6 feet of water can be fished with Road Runners and offset spinners. These baits are ideal for attracting the aggressive spring fish. These fish are in a protective/active mood that make them a prime target.

Fish spinners fast enough to allow the blade to work, yet slow like a crappie prefers. A very slow pull will let most baits fall gradually on the retrieve. A slow pull will keep baits at a consistent depth. A moderate speed will cause most blade baits to rise as they are retrieved. If crappie are showing a preference for a faster speed, a steady retrieve, mixed with occasional pauses will keep the bait at the level you desire while attracting extra strikes on the fall.

Don't be afraid to mix baits and presentations. Have one pole baited with a tube jig and another with an offset spinner. Switch outfits every few minutes to see what crappie like best. You may find both rigs work equally well.

FALL
Rating: 6

Fall is the time for crappie to move. They leave their summer homes and go to cooler, shallower water. A secondary ledge is a great place to find fall crappie.

Use the same techniques and baits as in the spring. The primary difference in presentation is that fall crappie may be more scattered than in the spring. They may be anywhere from a 4 foot depth to a 12 foot depth. Baits and presentations should be tailored to the depth being fished. For example, shallow water fish will more aggressively strike an offset spinner or curly tail retrieved at a moderate speed. Deeper fish will like a slow, more deliberate presentation with a tube or hair jig.

Fall fish are often heavy feeders. Crappie will be healthy and will put up a good fight.

SUMMER
Rating: 6

Summer secondary drops are difficult to rate. Most of the time depths will be too shallow for the extreme temperatures of summer. However, there are times when crappie will move to a secondary ledge and be easy to catch. Experience and spot-testing different locations is the best way to learn where and when secondary ledges in your local water are good.

Trolling is a top summer method in water 12 feet or less. Trolling keeps baits moving in the strike zone. Also, trolling keeps the fisherman cooler than locked in a stationary position. Other techniques: slowly bouncing minnows from the top to the bottom of the drop; slow trolling; and vertical jigging.

Very slow presentations call for minnows. Even when casting and dragging the bottom, a minnow is excellent in the summer.

Jigs are a suitable summer bait for secondary ledges. The jigs can be worked any depth and any speed. That's why trolling is such a great method for these baits. Use boat speed and jig weights to control depth.

Slow presentations need minnows. Even when casting and dragging the bottom, a minnow is excellent in the summer.

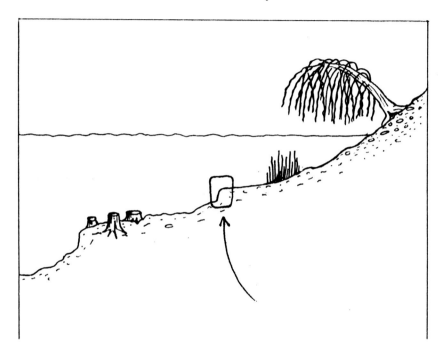

Secondary Ledge
A secondary ledge is more difficult to find, but can be a seasonal gold mine. As can be seen, a secondary ledge is usually not associated with a channel.

Vertical jigging with a pole held in each hand is another good technique. It lets you maintain contact with the bottom and cover to feel your way along the ledge. If fish are not on bottom, you can use your locator to stay with the ledge while you keep your baits at the right depth above the bottom.

WINTER
Rating: 5

If crappie are present on a secondary ledge, it's rated a "10". If temperatures keep them off of the ledge it is a "0". Therefore, the secondary ledge in the winter is a boom or bust situation. The best part is that it's quick to check for fish.

Techniques include slow trolling, vertical presentations or casting. These tactics are the way to successfully s-l-o-w fish a secondary ledge. Baits can be precisely positioned and fish found. Minnows are the slow bait of choice. They are hard to beat when held in front of a crappie's nose.

Jigs work, too. Bait speed is slow with action steady. Fish will sometimes like a jig to be hopping across the bottom, but most of the time jigs should be pulled slow and steady.

FACTORS
Secondary Ledges

*Cold Front -bad.
*Clouds/Rain -only minor changes.

Chapter 5

Creek/River Intersections

Open-water fishermen have learned that channels are used by fish as transportation routes. Fish use contours and channels similar to the way we use highways. Their interstates are the primary river channels; two lane highways are the smaller creek channels branching off of the primary channel; secondary roads are the tiny feeder creeks and ditches that branch off of the small channel.

Gravel roads and private drives are the structures breaking from any of these roads. For example, a private drive can be an old fence line, point, a cut in the channel, anything 'different' that can be used by a fish.

Creek/river intersections compare to our interstate/highway intersections. There's a lot of traffic on the interstate, a good number of vehicles on the two lane highway, but at the crossroad is a heavy traffic area because everything passes through that one point. It's the same situation at a creek/river intersection. Crappie travel the routes and swim through the intersections from different directions.

Seasonal Structure 54

Where are intersections found? In man-made lakes, reservoirs and river systems. Only a few natural and small manmade lakes will be void of channels.

Why fish intersections? They provide a place for you to catch fish that are holding on an intersection point or cover, but also gives you an opportunity to catch crappie on the move. Locating intersections is easy with a map and locator; difficult without a map; not practical without a locator. The map shows intersections that can be found by using landmarks. Points, coves and islands can be used to lineup the spot. A locator can be used to pinpoint the structure, contours and crappie where you can try your luck.

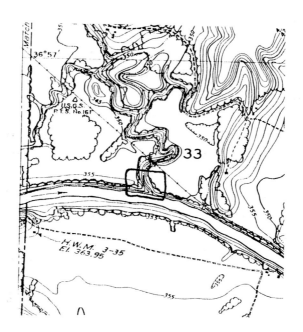

SUMMER
Rating: 10

The depths associated with summer vary greatly but generally have 25-50 feet of water available. Drop-offs will often be 15 feet or deeper.

Think about intersections for a moment. They have deep water, shallower water, drop-offs, points, slopes and cover; everything a fish could need or want. If the depths are right for a comfort zone, the intersections are perfect for crappie hangouts.

Cover is important on an intersection. These locations had trees or stumps when the lake was built because they were not flat enough to farm. Good natural cover is usually present. When natural cover isn't available, fishermen should sink wood cover (where legal) onto specific spots on the intersection.

Techniques for summer include slow trolling, vertical jigging, casting a free-fall jig, and minnows under slop-floats. Slow vertical trolling or jigging gets top pick for this structure. It allows fishermen to move along the drops and up and down the different depths. A fisherman can stair-step his approach to quickly find the proper depths and areas. Another advantage is the opportunity to check for fish on a locator while thoroughly fishing a spot.

Slow vertical techniques lets both minnow and jigs be fished. Minnows take top billing in the summer but both baits have a time and place.

Heavy double-hook rigs are good when going deep. A 3/4 ounce sinker will help to keep baits down. When using jigs, a 1/2 ounce primary weight along with a couple 1/32 or 1/16 ounce jigs is a good combo. Single jigs without a weight can be used, but stick to a 1/8 ounce head and move the boat very slowly to keep it from rising too much.

Tip: for using a 1/8 or even a 1/4 ounce jig; maintain a small hook size. For example, a 1/8 ounce jig is likely to have a heavy #1 hook designed for bass or walleye. However, a light wire #4 or #2 hook in the same size head will have several applications for crappie. (You may have to do some searching or even pour your own.)

WINTER
Rating: 10

Winter fishing gets a "10". Deep water being available makes intersections a top choice. Depth ranges should include water 25 feet or deeper for most waters.

Techniques for winter are very similar to summer. The key is to put baits on the fish. It may take time to find the right spots, but slow trolling or vertical jigging gives this option of searching while fishing.

Another technique worth mentioning is anchoring and casting. It lets a fisherman put his back to the wind and eliminates the work of boat control Open water intersections can be rough in the wind. A slip-float and minnow rig lets you fish any location that you want. If familiar with an area, a fisherman can anchor upwind from specific cover so the floats will stay directly in the cover.

Anchoring is also good for casting a jig. When depths are above 20 feet, casting a small 1/16 or 1/8 ounce jig to specific cover is excellent for slowly probing a spot and triggering fish. Take plenty of jigs with you when fishing deep wood cover.

SPRING
Rating: 7

Spring is a great time to catch crappie at intersections in 10 to 20 feet of water. Crappie use these spots during their late winter and early spring migration. Creek/creek intersections may be even better during the spirng.

Techniques vary a little when crappie use a wide range of depths. Crappie holding in schools in 12-18 feet can be

Travis Huffman with a nice, fat spring crappie.

caught with the winter and summer techniques previously described. Tactics change when they move up to shallower water on the points and flats associated with an intersection.

Fast trolling is good to quickly find and catch scattered fish. Once large numbers are found, switching to a technique to pinpoint a specific spot may be best.

The key is to match techniques to the crappie movements and depth. The same is true with baits. Tube jigs, curly tails, and Road Runners are good for casting or trolling in the spring. Don't be afraid to experiment with different types and colors to learn which ones they prefer.

Rigs can be a single hook rig instead of double. A large split-shot can be used above the minnow. These are good rigs for shallow depths.

FACTORS
Creek/River Intersections

***Wind** -no problem to the crappie.
***Strong Cold Front** -an intersection has the advantage of many depths for a comfort zone.
***Clouds/Rain** -ok.
***Sun** -ok, may move fish deeper.
***Fast Rise/Fall** -fish have plenty of depths to move into while
staying in the area.
***Current** -a problem, but crappie will get tight to cover and away from strong current.
***High Water** -fish will suspend over the same structure they were on or they will move shallower.

FALL
Rating: 6

Fall intersection fishing is much the same as it is in the spring. There will be numbers of fish; all on the move. They hold in deeper water but quickly move up and down to feed on drops, flats, etc. Depths change daily and even from hour to hour.

The key is to find the active depth. Keep an open mind because you may catch fish at 9 feet in the morning and then the action stops. It doesn't mean that fish have quit biting, but they have probably moved to a different depth. So remember, sunlight and bait locations are very important.

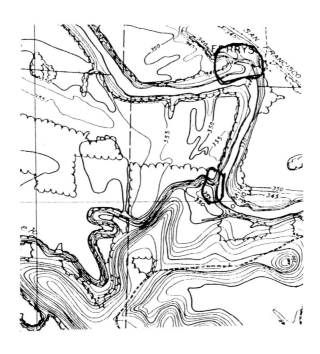

Seasonal Structure

Section 2
Man-Made Structures
Three Top Picks

-Concrete Bridge Pilings
-Rocky Banks
-Floating Docks

Chapter 6

Concrete Bridge Pilings

Day or night, bridge pilings are a popular place for crappie anglers. These pilings are magnets for hundreds of fish.

The depth range in stained waters is 0-30 feet. Although a piling may be any depth, the practical fishing depths are within certain ranges. Muddy waters and/or shallow lakes: 0-12 feet, clear waters: 0-50.

Why fish a piling? Concrete attracts algae; algae draws baitfish: baitfish draw crappie. Another attractor is the normally warmer temperatures around a concrete column. Last, but not least, is the current break. Since creeks and rivers are associated with most bridges, current is present.

There are no secrets to finding pilings. Any type of bridge of crossing in the lake is a location with pilings. Ask local fishermen. Look at the topo map. Visually scout the lake.

Seasonal Structure   64

WINTER
Rating: 9

Winter is the ideal time to fish concrete. Sun warms the exposed concrete which radiates heat down into the submersed concrete. This concrete then warms the water in direct contact with the piling. The result can be water that's a few tenths up to a few degrees warmer than surrounding water. This makes it a prime winter/ late winter fishing spot!

There are many tactics that will work to catch piling crappie. A favorite of many fishermen is to cast. This can be done from an anchored boat or one controlled in a trolling motor. Another technique is to tightline jigs up, down, and along a piling. This technique gives a slower presentation than casting and is suitable for most situations.

A third method is minnows under a float. Deep water requires a slip-float, but it makes fishing a very simple task.

Crappie may be anywhere along a piling, but there are a few special locations where they are likely to hold. This is important to know so you can fish wisely. This means fishing the right technique and placing the bait in front of the fish.

The best thing you can do to eliminate time is to locate crappie using your electronics. This gives you a very good idea of where and how deep.

The first place to look is beside the piling. Its location is dependent upon current, depth, and temperatures. Dragging a bait along the side will likely trigger these fish.

The second place to find crappie is on the downstream side of the piling. They'll be very close on a small piling, but may be some distance back on a big concrete support. The water immediately behind the piling creates a small eddy; slack water for a crappie to hold. Small baitfish are swept into the eddy giving crappie plenty of good food to eat.

Casting to a piling lets you control depth, speed and action. Start your retrieves in the upper depths gradually working down on the next cast. Bump the concrete. This attracts the fish. It also flakes algae off the concrete and excites fish. Try steady retrieves so you can stay in contact with the bait. If that doesn't work, try pumping actions or small hops. Try different things to trigger strikes.

Tightlining and minnow/float fishing are different methods. Fewer movements are needed to the baits. The important thing is to watch closely for bites and know exactly where your baits are at all times so you can catch more fish from the same spot.

FALL
Rating: 8

Fall crappie are on the move but they don't ignore a piling. There are usually a number of fish that will be holding at a piling, waiting for a meal.

The tactics include casting or long poling. It's the same as in winter except fish may be shallower.

SPRING
Rating: 6

Any structure will attract spring crappie. A piling in early spring has many advantages including the heating effect of the concrete.

Spring crappie will be caught in typical locations. A little trial and error may be required to find just the right spot. The rule of thumb is to fish the down-current side of a piling when current is moderate to strong; beside and directly behind the piling when there is little or no current.

SUMMER

Rating: 6

Summer is different than the other seasons because the concrete can sometimes be a disadvantage. Pilings are such good structures that fish will still use them, but the crappie will be selective in choosing where they stay. Shadow areas and night fishing are two keys for summer pilings.

In the daytime, the shady areas should be fished first. Check each section of the piling to find a pattern. Don't forget the downcurrent side.

Stick with small jigs in the summer. Casting gives more versatility and is fun.

Night fishing is a great tactic. You can avoid overcrowded lakes and the heat.

Night fishing requires a little preparation. Not having a flashlight in the boat, inability to find the landing net when a big one hits, and not having insect repellent are a few examples of poor planning which can ruin a trip. Making a checklist will help you to remember important items.

Lights are important tools, too. Two types lf lighting are lanterns and floating lights. To oversimplify: light attracts bugs and insects; bugs attract baitfish; baitfish attract crappie.

Anchoring is your first task upon arriving at a piling. Anchoring is accomplished by placing the front anchor far in front of the boat on the upstream side. The rope is fed until the boat is over the correct location. The boat is positioned as desired and the back anchor dropped. Always start on the downstream side of a piling.

Placing lights is next. Strong poles are used to hold lanterns out of the water and away from the boat.

Minnow buckets, landing nets, flashlights and poles should be placed in easy-to-reach locations.

Fishing begins. Vertical tightlining is the preferred night-time presentation. Long rods rigged with minnows are ideal to fish around the light. Extra-long poles are cumbersome; short poles limit fishing to beside the boat.

Depths for catching piling crappie under the lights can vary from 10 to 60 feet. However, pilings in most fishing lakes are in 20 feet of water or less.

Summer, night-time fishing is either 'feast or famine'. Patience is critical. Once the action starts, every pole in the boat will be bending. A school of fish moving through the lights is an exciting event you won't soon forget.

FACTORS
Concrete Bridge Pilings

***Wind** -you can often get on the backside of pilings for a windbreak.
***Strong Front** -fish become negative.
***Clouds/Rain** -not usually a problem; can even help fishermen by putting a roof over his head.
***Sun** -helps to warm pilings during cold weather; it pushes fish to the shady side in hot weather.
***Current** -puts fish on the downstream side of the pil-

MORE ON CONCRETE PILINGS
Subject Expert: Wally Marshall

Lake Fork, Texas, crappie guide Wally Marshall has a lot of experience fishing bridge pilings. He has some different ideas to share about these good structures.

The pilings I fish are big, round concrete pilings that go from the bridge down to the bottom and then some. They're about 36 inches in diameter. Most bridges have three pilings together and some have two. Every bridge is different.

Many have a crossmember 10-15 feet below the surface. This holds the pilings together. This is a 3' by 3' concrete crossmember.

Marshall believes that approach is very important. Crappie move up and down depending upon temperatures and light penetration. Also, he says they're chasing bait around the piling because the shad like to feed off of the algae and zooplankton. The crappie are after shad.

High sun sends crappie down. The crossmember provides them with shade and protection. In the spring, they'll actually spawn on the support members.

I cast parallel to the cross member. When the lure pendulums down, it covers every depth. Once it gets to the right depth, "boom", you'll get a strike. Make another cast and count down to the same depth where you caught the fish and start slow reeling."

Marshall's equipment includes a Wally Marshall signature series 5'6" light action that has a lot of backbone with a light tip. Here he likes to use this rod to shoot jigs in tight places under a bridge. He usually uses a shooting technique because it's easy, efficient, and the rod won't be broken by accidentally slamming the tip into the top of a bridge, piling, or cross structure.

His line is Berkley 6 lb test Trilene XL spooled on a Quantum Iron reel.

His rig includes two, 1/32 ounce Road Runners 14 inches apart. *The tandem combination covers two depths and gives me the chance to catch two at a time.*

My retrieve is a pendulum drop with a slow, steady retrieve after a countdown.

Final Tips:

Crappie will spawn on the crossmembers. Remember to fish all portions thoroughly. They'll be on the pilings away from the creek channel on the shallowest bridge at this time.

Crappie will move to the deeper pilings in the summer and winter.
Spring is deadly; a home run. Summer is a base hit. Fall is good; a double. Winter is poor.

Wally Marshall at the 1997 Crappie USA Classic. He and his partner had a great 2nd place finish in the two-day event.

Chapter 7

Man-Made Rocky Banks

There are lots of places to find man-made rocky structures. One of the most common is along earthen dams where rocks have been placed to prevent erosion. Another place is where rocks are dumped on a bank to prevent it from erosion (examples include bridges, roads, railroad tracks.) Dikes or wake walls are another man-made structure where excellent fishing can take place during the right water conditions. Look for rocks in both small and huge impoundments.

Why fish the rocks? Because fish like them. There are several reasons for this with the first one being temperature. When water is cool, a few days of sunshine will warm the rocks making them a solar panel. In turn, this warms the surrounding water. This is dynamite in the spring.

Another reason: rocks are a primary structure used by baitfish. Different baits move and hide in the rocks. Crappie won't be too far behind when baitfish move into an area.

Unless the water is completely over rocks, they can be visually located. Also, a topo map will usually show areas where rocks are likely to be. With experience, you can pick out those areas.

Manmade Rocky Areas

- Wake walls ...to protect areas from natural and barge-created waves.

- Rip-Rap along dirt banks ...to protect area from washing away.

- Near bridges ..protecting from erosion.

- Along earthen dams and roads ...to stop waves from damaging and washing.

- Beside launching ramps.

- Big dikes on rivers.

- Rock walls along private property bordering water.

- Underwater house foundations, bridges and railroad beds.

- Near and around marina areas.

SPRING
Rating: 9

Rocks are an important spring structure because of the heating effect. Sun and warm breezes warm the rocks and therefore, the water. Top early season picks are in coves (as compared to main lake areas). Wake walls are good because they provide a wind break and they gather a lot of sun. North and northwest rocky areas are likely to be the best because they will receive the most sun and warm southerly breezes.

Techniques vary with depth. Water 15 feet or greater is best fished with vertical tightlining methods. Fishing vertically gives the best control and keeps baits in the strike zone. When fish are up a little, casting a jig is best. Shallow fish can be caught using a jig and float while fish in the 10 to 15 foot range needs a free-fall jig.

A free-fall jig allows more versatility and depths can be controlled with a countdown method. Casts are made from a trolling motor controlled boat, working different locations until crappie are found. Then casts can be concentrated in a specific area. Hit the spot hard until the fish stop biting. You can leave and come back later to catch more. It's important to move until fish are found because fall fish are normally active and feeding if present.

Another advantage of using a free-fall jig and working different locations is fun. There's nothing like having a jig tic the rocks occasionally and then have a big slab inhale it.

When presenting jigs on the rocks use slow or medium speed. For example, on bottom they want a very slow jig. In shallower water where their metabolisms are faster, they may want a faster bait. The easiest way to determine how is to use a slower retrieve as you increase the depth. Increase your speeds slightly as you catch more fish; they'll let you know when you must slow a bait down.

Deep and mid depth baits can be tubes or any standard jig. Shallow water fish may prefer a curly tail and/or a small spinner.

SUMMER

Rating: 8

Summer rocks are a hit and miss situation. The most likely time to catch fish along the deeper rocks is at night. Summer night fishing has always been a popular tactic.

One reason fish may not be around rocks is due to the

Fishing a rock dike on a large river can produce big numbers of crappie. Which dike? First choice is one below an oxbow lake.

heat of the sun transferred through the rocks. This is a negative when the water is already hot.

The number one area for early to mid summer is along mid-depth rocks beside bridges. Crappie need deep water nearby; bridges are built over channels. Fish are likely to move up and down from the channel into the rocks.

Another good area is a dike. A dike provides a current shelter. The fish enjoy just getting behind a dike to rest and feed. They are comfortable along a rocky dike. Major rivers provide excellent dike opportunities. During high water the dikes have large holes washed out behind them. The large holes are excellent places to fish when the water goes down.

Tip: when major flooding has occurred, the water will wash fish into and out of the oxbow lakes along the river. Oxbows can be good, but more importantly, dikes just downstream from oxbows are excellent in the summer following floods. Hit the dikes below the oxbows.

Presentations are about the same as in the spring. Minnows may become more important in the summer. Give the fish both and let them decide. Trolling can be used when fish are scattered.

FALL

Rating: 5

The quality of fishing along the rocksdepends upon crappie movements and will rank from 1 to 8. Fall feeding binges make some structures excellent when conditions are right. Rocks are used because they are a structure located in an area where fish like to be, not because the fish travel to a spot just to get to the rocks.

Aggressive techniques are good in the fall. Casting or trolling is highly recommended. Baits should be kept moving in high percentage areas to locate fish. Fall fish will usually bite so finding them is the key. The rule of thumb is: move fast; don't stay in one spot if the fish aren't there; once found, slow down and work the area hard.

Specific fall baits along the rocks include: curly tail jigs, hard plastic minnows like the AWD Crappie Firetail Delight; and offset spins like the Johnson Beetle Spin.

Winter Tip: Check for suspended crappie around rocks. Rocks at 25 feet may have fish suspending at 16 feet. Pay attention to the locator and be sure not to fish below all of the fish. Baits should be about a foot above the fish.

WINTER
Rating: 4

A rating of 4 can be misleading because every situation is different and may produce great fishing or nothing at all. Water depth is a key in the winter. Also, the heating effect of the rocks can be a minor factor. It's a simple fact that fish like rocks, so when they are at a proper depth crappie are likely to be present.

The way to go after winter crappie in the 18 to 30 foot range is by slow vertical trolling. This also means vertical tightlining. Casting a jig deep is difficult when there's current.

Rocks eat sinkers. Have plenty of rigs whether tightlining minnows or jigs. Try to keep baits just above the rocks.

These rocks are protecting gravesites along the river portion of a lake. Rocky banks like these can be good structure and includes deep water.

FACTORS
Man-Made Rocky Banks

***Wind** -depends upon the velocity and direction vs location of the rocks.

***Clouds/Rain** -usually a good factor for scattering fish making trolling long stretches of rocks very productive.

***Sun** -good in cold weather.

***Fast Rise/Fall** -ok at most rocky areas because fish can easily adjust depths and stay on the rocks.

***Current** -not good because hiding places are often not available in and around rock banks.

***High Water** -must test fish, but can be good.

***Fishing Pressure** -some rock areas are fished very hard and can lessen the enjoyment and productivity of the spot.

Chapter 8

Floating Docks

A good depth range below a dock is 10 to 30 feet. Slope, water conditions and cover all play a part in the best fish-holding spots.

Docks are everywhere (almost). They provide walkways and a place to secure a boat. A dock may hold one or fifty boats. They are built on lakes and rivers where the water fluctuates. (Lakes kept relatively constant use more driven-post, stationary docks.)

Waters, where privately owned land boarders the shoreline, is another big factor. Private landowners will build docks for private use while the Corp of Engineer lakes will have public land adjoining the water without docks.

High-use recreation lakes have the most floating docks. Lake of the Ozarks, Missouri, is one example. Huge cruisers, hundreds of jet skies, party barges and ski boats all need a place to park when not in use. Floating docks provide a garage for these boats.

Why fish? Because a floating dock is structure. It provides shade, a variety of water depths (if it's a good fishing dock) and some form of bottom structure.

Finding a dock is easy. Just look.

Once found, a contour map and locator become critical. A good year-round dock will have plenty of depth. Shallow water docks should be avoided when deeper ones are available. Before fishing, make a pass around to check depth, drops, and cover.

A floating dock also can have a roof. This feature not only protects a boat from the elements, it also provides more shade for fish.

SUMMER
Rating: 9

Floating docks are particularly good in the hot summer. Fish are less scattered; they're located in cooler, shaded areas.

Two methods for shooting for fishing docks are shooting and longpoling. The first is shooting. Shooting docks is a method to place jigs into tight places. Roofs, cables, and ropes are easier to avoid with shooting tactics. Jigs can be launched in a straight line directly to the target.

Shooting isn't easy but it can be learned. A 5 or 5.5 foot long rod is needed. A spinning reel is the best choice, but a smooth closed-face can be used, too. The bait is a jig; usually a 1/32 ounce.

Shooting is performed by holding the bait between your thumb and forefinger. Always hold the leadhead with the hook in a safe position.

The jig is pulled to cause the rod to arc. When the jig reaches the front of the handle (depending upon rod stiffness)

83 *Floating Docks*

Crappie expert and Weiss Lake guide Sam Heaton uses the shooting method to reach the backs of docks without

the rod is loaded and ready to fire.

The rod is aimed and the jig is 'shot' toward the selected target. Practice is required to correctly control the up/down trajectory. Because the rod arc is always 90 degrees to the surface of the water, left to right direction is seldom a problem.

Shooting lets a jig be placed in the back of a stall even when a boat only leaves a space of a few inches. Another place is between floatation blocks. The Crappiethon Classic winners at Lake Hamilton, Hot Springs, Arkansas, laid on the boat deck and shot jigs between the blocks of styrofoam under the walkways. This put their jigs under the walk and into the stall on the opposite side. The retrieve brought baits from the light into the shade and back into the light.

The second method is long poling. A 12 or 14 foot pole is good for a dock without roof while an 8 or 10 foot pole is used for docks with a roof.

Fishing techniques are similar to fishing other structures. A bait can be flipped or vertical jigged in all of the dock openings. The disadvantage is the restriction to some areas of a dock. Getting between styrofoam or other tight places make hook-setting difficult or impossible.

It's important to know which general lake areas and specific dock spots to fish. The first rule is to have deep water available under the dock. Deep water is critical. The depth variations give a comfort zone and plenty of protection.

The next rule is: more shade equals more fish. Shade is the reason summer crappie locate in that structure. A roof, pontoon or other object used to provide shade is a positive factor.

Specific dock areas are determined by light penetration, water conditions, underwater contours and cover. The general theory is to fish the shadiest spots. However, it's common to find crappie using the shade/shadow breakline for a holding spot. Therefore, fish all available water at different depths until a pattern is found.

SPRING
Rating: 7

The majority of crappie move shallow in the spring. This includes shallow spawning beds and mid-depth staging areas. Docks with submerged structure can be very good, especially when scattered at various depths. Unlike other seasons, fish will be more 'cover/depth' oriented than specifically using the floating dock. In other words, good contour depths and cover would provide spring fishing with or without a dock.

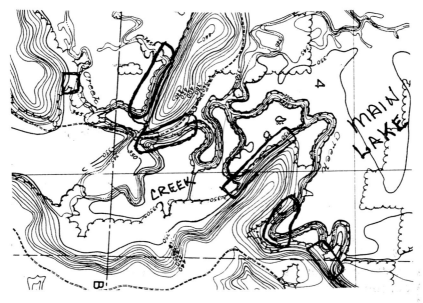

The best docks are located in and/or near deep water. The spots marked are ideal areas for a dock.

FALL
Rating: 6

Fish are often on the move and actively feeding in the fall. Docks are still a great spot to catch fish when sunlight and other factors hold them below in the shadows.

WINTER
Rating: 4

This can be a 10 rating at some docks with proper depth and plenty of wood cover. A heated dock is a prime example of a deepwater, cover saturated crappie hangout. Other docks may be a zero in the winter. Since shade isn't so important to comfort in the winter and can even be a negative, a floating dock has little to offer.

FACTORS
Floating Docks

***Strong Cold Front** -usually ok if enough depth is present.
***Clouds/Rain** -bad; scatters fish away from docks.
***Sun** -very good.
***Muddy/Clear Water** -clear is best because light penetration will be a bigger influence to drive fish under the docks.
***Fishing Pressure** -docks will only hold a limited number of active fish; more fishermen means fewer fish available.
***Boat Traffic** -might drive a few openwater fish into the docks. It makes fishing docks extremely difficult and dangerous.

MORE ON FLOATING DOCKS
Subject Expert: Guy Winters

Guy Winters is a seminar speaker, vice president of Laker Lures and crappie expert. He has a home lake loaded with small, medium and huge floating docks. Lake of the Ozarks in Missouri, has been his testing ground for many different fishing situations involving these floating structures. His knowledge and experience can provide us with valuable information and tips.

What is a floating dock?

It's a structure that's supported by some type of floatation. The space between the dock and water never changes. They range in size from a single weld to sixty welds. We have a lot of large floating docks on Lake of the Ozarks; many resorts and marinas.

How about dock size vs. fishing?

Fishing is directly related to the people using the dock, not the physical size of it. I've found that docks without any structure whatsoever results in poor fishing, unless it's positioned near a spring coming into the lake. A dock by itself will hold fish during high, bluebird days but that's about the only time. You must have brush.

How do you read a dock?

I always look to see what kind of boat is in the dock. If it's a fishing boat then I look for a cleaning station. If it has a cleaning station, I know the guy is a fisherman.

The next thing I look for is rod holders and lights. This tells me which side of the dock brush is on. I also look in the well of the dock to see if there are any cables hanging down with suspended brush. These things say "Premier dock".

Seasonal Structure

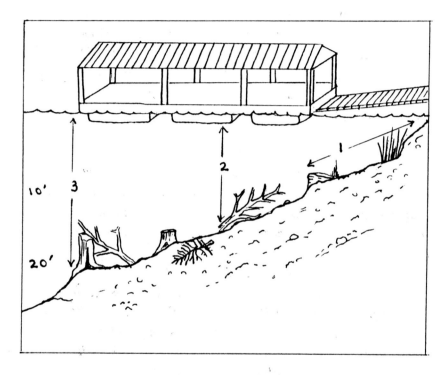

Floating Dock Seasonal Patterns
1. Spring and Fall; shallow water.
2. All seasons; typical comfort zone.
3. Summer and Winter; fish may be anywhere from the the top to the deeper bottom, most likely deep.

You've visually checked the dock. Now what?

I run by the dock with the trolling motor. My eyes are on the locator looking for brush and structure. Also, depending upon the time of year, I need to know depth.

What depth is needed?

A dock with 20 feet of water has the possibility of being a good year-round dock. It depends upon the bank behind it. If the bank slopes gradually, has pea gravel, brush at all depths, that dock will hold fish basically all year, especially if it's close to the main channel. You need the right depth, a channel and brush.

Winters' tips for locating the best docks:
1. Topo map; stay on the shoreline closest to a channel.
2. Good visual inspection of the dock.
3. Scan edges with LCR

What about seasonal aspects of fishing a dock?

Temperature triggers movements. The early spring feeding binge starts at 50 degrees. Crappie can be found at 8 or 10 feet.

At 60 degrees they may be as shallow as 2 feet. At 62 thru 69, the females come in. Once finished, they start their migration back out at the rate of 1 to 1.5 feet per degree rise in temperature.

They are active and feeding. They want cover so a dock with a sloping bottom and cover is a perfect place for year-round crappie including spring.

In 86 to 87 degrees, you will normally have fish at 20 to 25 feet. A dock changes their position some because of the light penetration into the water. All fish are light sensitive. A fish at 20 feet without a dock may be as shallow as 8 feet under a dock.

Guy says the fall pattern is similar to the spring but less

exaggerated in depths. Winter is different because the shade can be a negative factor. However, deep brush should still hold fish.
How do you fish a dock?
Fishing deeper than 8 feet requires vertical jigging tactics. I can move a jig slow and subtle. I drop the jig to the bottom and let it set for a count of 5. I then bring it up 6 inches and hold it there. I bring it up six inches each time. I'll hold my line and just twitch it with my fingers. That's all the action I give it. I watch my line to know when a fish picks it up.

For fish less than 8 feet, I pitch. I hold the rodtip at 11 o'clock and let the bait fall back toward me. If that doesn't work, I'll use a cast and retrieve.

I switch to a 5.5 foot stiff rod for fish 15 feet or deeper. Fish at that depth don't hold on for long. To catch a fish, you've got to load the rod, stretch the line, and drive the hook through the fish's mouth. That takes time. I just eliminate loading the rod. The result is a quicker hookset.

Equipment?
All spinning rods. A 7.5 foot in less than 8 feet of water; a 6.5 with a fast tip and heavy butt in 8 to 15 feet; and 5.5 foot when deeper than 15 feet.

I've not fished with a minnow for 30 years. Plastic 1.5 and 2 inch tube jigs are excellent baits. I also like a Curly Bug. It's similar to a curly tail grub with wings on the side of it. I like it because it doesn't fall straight down. A Paddle Bug is good, too. Both can be worked slowly.

Section 3
Wood Structures

-Manmade Wood
-Stumps, Snags, & Logs
-Fallen Trees (Laydowns)

Chapter 9

Manmade Wood Structure

Crappie and bass guides, tournament fishermen, and serious anglers have placed cover in lakes for many years. They know the importance of having cover in key locations. It's cover they have available that the weekend fishermen seldom find.

Manmade structures are not fun to make or place. It takes time and hard work. So why make and place wood cover in a lake where natural wood exist? Because new structures can be placed where they are best for the crappie. They also replenish the ever-deteriorating natural wood improving the overall condition of a lake. The best personal reason is that structures become a good place for you to catch crappie. It's 'your' crappie hole; not because you have more rights to it, but because it will be fished by fewer fishermen because they won't know its location.

Manmade cover isn't limited to a specific type of tree or bed. A popular bed is made from a wooden shipping pallet. Boards 3 to 5 feet long are nailed into the pallet in an upright position. Boards (stakes) number 15 to 30 per pallet. Once completed, the pallet can be sunk in a strategic position by using concrete blocks at each corner. Two pallets placed together are considered a good size bed (4x8 ft.).

Seasonal Structure

Man-Made Wood Structures
•top left: Brush; Limbs; or Wooded Poles placed in buckets or plastic conatiners and then filled with concrete.
•top right: Pallet with boards nailed upright. A concrete block at each corner can be used.
•bottom left: Evergreen (Christmas tree). Sunk by tying onion sacks full of rocks to it.
•bottom right: Large Limb or Small Tree. Weight added to sink.

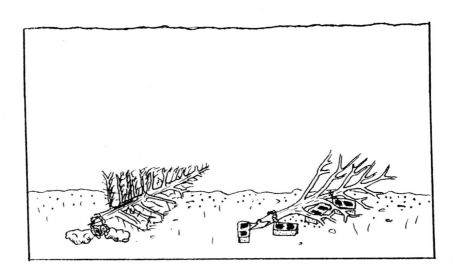

A better way to make a stakebed is to drive stakes directly into the ground. This is done when the lake is at a low level. Stakes should be about 8 inches apart, 3 to 6 feet tall, and number 40 to 100 stakes. A bed made like this will be excellent and tough.

Another excellent structure is brush piles. Although the brush is natural, sinking them firmly to the bottom in good locations makes them manmade. Top covers include hickory, birch and hedge apple. Hardwoods are best because they last longer. Brush and small trees can be sunk by tying concrete blocks or rocks to them.

Softwoods work but decay quicker than hardwoods. Another popular tree to sink is an evergreen. Christmas tree evergreens are good to place because there's nothing better to do with them. However, they take time to start working and are not a favorite of the man-made structure pros.

Sink cover at proper depths. The key depth is 15 feet (20 to 25 feet in clear water), but depths, anywhere from 10 to 20 feet in a stained lake can give good results. The cover needs to work throughout all the seasons, so deeper water does this while keeping the beds well below the surface for safety purposes. Look for places like points, drops and flats. The less natural cover, the better manmade cover will be.

Sinking cover is hard work and is dangerous. Use a safe boat, lifejacket and work with a partner. Also, check local lake laws to insure they allow cover to be placed.

Finding cover placed by others is another way to fish. There's nothing wrong with it. No bed belongs to the person who sinks it. With today's electronics and the knowledge of fishermen, it's impossible to hide all of the beds. Beds can be found around obvious places including boat docks, points and on ledges.

SPRING
Rating: 10

Spring beds are excellent fishing. They provide crappie a home as they move along their migration to and from shallow water. Beds in 8 to 15 feet of water are best in the spring. It's important to note that spring is a time when a bed may be good one day and not the next, because of the rapid changes taking place in the spring. However, with beds at different locations and depths, some will surely produce.

Driven stakebed made during low water will pay big dividends when the water returns to normal pool.

Beds in the spring are intended for staged crappie. Stained water fish will probably not spawn as deep as the beds, but every lake is different so there are no solid rules.

There are many techniques that can be successfully used in stakebeds. A straight up and down method is popular with many fishermen because it gives them maximum control. Depths, timing and small movements are easy to handle.

Casting to stakebeds is also a popular tactic. Casting lets a fisherman maintain a distance from the bed to avoid spooking fish. A float keeps the depth constant and allows for any speed, including no movement at all.

Wooden manmade board, tree or wood/plastic structures are similar to stakebeds. The same techniques and tactics can be used.

Brush piles are different. Small limbs enjoy grabbing every hook that enters their zone. Vertical jigging is the best practical way to fish the piles. Minnow hooks should be weedless or be prepared to replace them frequently.

Baits and presentations are basic. Minnows should be about 2.5-3.0 inches long and jigs 2.0 inches. Present vertically or by casting under a float. Few movements or tricks are needed.

SUMMER/WINTER
Rating: 10

Fish are generally in the same areas and depths during both seasons. Water/weather conditions will determine whether they are in 10, 15, 20, or 25 feet of water.

Why fish these seasons? Because crappie move to deep ledges. Dropped cover in areas they use will draw them into it. The cover then becomes a spot for a fisherman to target.

Where are the fish? A typical lake during winter and

Seasonal Structure

Cover is often where you find it and how creative you are at building it. These are two small brush piles built by Tim and Chatt Martin. This brush can be carried to other lakes for a quick drop-off holding spot. They are also good for creating a long 'fence row' from a ledge to a shallower structure like a dock or fallen tree.

summer, most fish will be in 15 to 20 feet of water. Water clarity and other factors come into play.

Casting a 1/16 or 1/8 ounce jig is good in the summer and winter. A cast can be made, letting the jig sink to the bottom, and then retrieved very slowly. This retrieve catches fish, lets a fisherman know what is on bottom and reveals the depths where the casts are being made.

Vertical tighlining is an excellent method, especially in deeper water. Minnow or jigs can be used. S-l-o-w is the key when moving baits.

FALL
Rating: 6

Fall has a lower rating but man-made structures are still one of the best structures to fish. Due to fish moving a lot in the fall, fewer fish are likely to be in any particular bed or brush pile.

Vertical fishing tactics will work, but casting is the best pick here. Jigs with a lot of action should be used.

FACTORS
Manmade Wood Structure

***Wind** -carefully placed cover can insure that you can have a windbreak no matter which direction the wind blows.
***Strong Front** -cover at different depths help when conditions are tough.
***Sun** -strong sunlight will send crappie tight to cover.
***Current** -cover holds crappie when currents are present.
***Fishing Pressure** -with today's electronics and others watching you pull fish prevents you from totally concealing your crappie homes. However, fewer fishermen will find them than other covers that's available.

Seasonal Structure

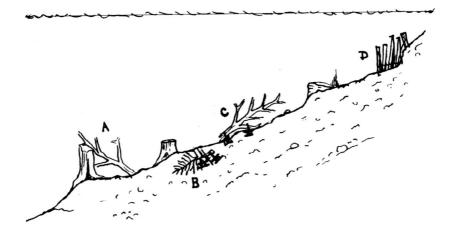

Placement of Wood Cover

A. Stump: natural wood cover. Limb may be a drifter or placed by a fisherman.
B. Christmas Tree: evergreen sunk with concrete blocks.
C. Small Tree or Large Limb: sunk by using concrete blocks and/or rocks.
D. Driven Stakebed: 2x2's, 1x4's, similar wood pieces.

    The logical depth for a bed in a stained lake is 15 feet (+/- 3 feet) for year-round wood. The top of the cover will be around 6-12 feet.
    Driven stakebed should be placed during low water levels to give the bed a better depth during normal water levels.

DROPPING COVER

The type of trees used to make brush piles are important. Hickory and birch are top picks for cover. The hardwoods last longer and make a good home for fish. Hedge apple and fruit trees are another option.

Softwoods work too, but will not last as long as hardwoods. Christmas trees (pines, cedars, etc.) make cover and is better than just burning them, but are the least desirable of the group. Evergreens shouldn't be dropped until they have died.

Quick Outline:
1. Find the area to drop cover. This should be a location that has crappie but very little cover. Look in areas 15 to 20 feet deep.
2. Search the area thoroughly with a locator. Pinpoint the spot you like and drop a buoy.
3. Next, get the cover.
    Size notes:
Small areas of brush will draw fish and are difficult for other people to find. (They may be hard for you to find, too!).
A midsize area is recommended. A 4x8 foot area is just right.
A large bed or pile may or may not draw more fish. It will be found by other fishermen after they see you pulling in fish.
4. Drive stakes into the bottom or sink the cover. Concrete blocks and/or rocks can be used. It takes more weight than you might think to sink and settle a lot of wood.
5. Bait the pile or bed. Alfalfa pellets draw minnows; minnows draw fish. It will speed up the use of the spot you create.
6. Before retrieving the buoy, note all the landmarks necessary to return to the exact spot. Write them down in a book.

Note: Dropping cover and baiting is illegal in some waters. Check your local laws.

Chapter 10

Stumps, Snags & Logs

There's nothing more obvious than a stump sticking out of the water. It's a calling card that attracts fishermen. Experience has taught us that a crappie or two will likely be next to the stump.

A stump provides protection from predators, wind, waves, and gives crappie an ambush spot. If a single stump, it's isolated cover meaning that if fish are in the area they'll be on the stump. A row of stumps gives more cover for larger numbers of fish.

There are two types of stumps: visible and submerged. Both are good cover but have different characteristics.

Stumps can be at any depth. The season will determine the depth to search for fish.

Where are stumps found? In almost any waters. Man-made lakes have stumps if the area was logged; standing trees if not logged. Fields and home sites were cleared. The natural stumps are good because they are permanent from year to year. Deep, natural lakes are the least likely to have stumps.

Logs are different because they change locations. They drift, float, lodge and settle. But without a doubt, a log is an excellent crappie home. It's important to keep these locations in mind when searching for fish.

Why fish stumps or logs? Wood and crappie go together like mom, apple pie and America. Wood has all the properties needed to hold crappie.

Some topo maps are excellent for giving locations of underwater covers including stumps and standing trees. Maps can be used as a guideline to start stump fishing.

Visible stumps are no problem to find. A locator is a necessity for finding deep stumps. It shows where the stumps are located, even when it's in areas you don't expect to find them. Trolling and drifting are excellent fish-catching tactics allowing a fisherman to search for wood while fishing.

A third method for finding wood is with a hook. Exact stump and log locations are found using a double-hook bottom bouncer or by casting a jig. Repeated presentations to the spot without getting hung will produce fish if they are there.

There is one more type of stump, too. This is the one dreaded by all boaters. The one that's almost visible. This stump is a safety hazard, but can be a dynamite fishing spot. The best ones are those usually visible only as a dark spot in the water. The ones hard to find are not going to have as much fishing pressure as the visible stumps.

What's a snag? It's nothing more than a tall stump. Snags are fished similar to a stump. The primary difference is that more of it is sticking out of the water than a stump. Snags down below the water level offers a wide range of depth in which to search for crappie.

Stumps, Snags & Logs

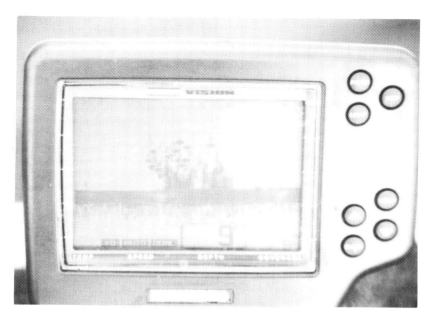

Stumps, snags, logs and other wood structure should hold fish as seen here on the locator.

SPRING

Rating: 10

Stumps in 8, 10, 12 and 15 feet of water are excellent in stained water lakes (deeper in clear lakes). These underwater stumps are top holding spots for pre-spawn and post-spawn crappie. In clear water they'll even be in spawning depths.

Better early springtime stumps or snags may be the visual ones. Exposed wood will act as a solar collector. Any small difference in temperature is very important in cold water. Later in the season it's not a factor. But a visible stump should never be ignored.

Techniques for fishing stumps, snags and logs can be

slow trolling, fast trolling, pulling or casting. The best methods will be dictated by the ability to get and keep baits in the stumps without staying hung-up.

A good-any-time method is vertical jigging with long poles. Tightlining allows a jig to be placed against wood cover and works at all depths. It's a perfect wood technique for all situations.

Tube jigs are excellent to use around visible stumps. They have good action; colors are easy to change; they can be presented next to wood in a realistic manner.

To work a snag or stump, work a jig slowly downward. For example, a five foot deep stump (snag) should be fished by dropping the jig to one foot and holding for five seconds. Drop down another foot and hold; continuing until all depths are fished. Drop the jig on the opposite side and repeat the process.

The same technique can be used for fishing minnows.

Catch the top fish first using either jigs or minnows. This will cause the least disturbance to other fish. Once a depth pattern is established, keep baits within a foot or two of the best depth. Time can be saved by not fishing above or below the strike zone.

Pitching is another good technique to use around visible stumps and logs. This is performed by pitching a bait past the stump and letting it pendulum down along the side of the wood. The pendulum swing is a slow fall, slow swim past the wood. It covers different depths while presenting the bait with a very crappie-like motion.

Tip: Let your bait bump into the side of limbs and the main part of a stump, snag or log. This won't spook crappie when using small weights. It will draw their attention to the bait.

Guide Norm Trautman ties to a snag and proceeds to methodically vertical jig all of the wood cover at all depths. This tactic has paid big dividends for he and his clients.

WINTER

Rating: 10

Deep stumps are the most likely to hold large numbers of concentrated fish. What's deep? It's relative to the body of water but is in the 18-30 foot range on typical stained waters. Deep is good because many of the stumps left will be along drops, ledges and steep slopes.

One method for catching these fish is a tightlining

Kentucky Lake Rig or heavy jigs. It can be to your advantage to mark the stump or log when fishing these structures. Throw the buoy 10 feet away from the stump. Hang on for a lot of action.

The Kentucky Lake rig can be dropped along the sides and on top of the wood. The rig is good for knowing what's under the water including cover, slope and bottom type. Winter is a good time to vary minnow sizes.

Jigs can be any type. Weight is important because light jigs will take too long to get down. Heavy jigs are good but have less natural action. A 1/16 ounce jig with a small split-shot is about right. A 1/8 ounce jig is also a good choice.

Bait speed should be slow to super-slow. Don't be quick to move the bait. Give them plenty time to look, smell and decide if they want it. Strike quick on a hit.

Tip: A superline is excellent in deep water. It's more sensitive. A fisherman can feel cover and strikes. Low stretch gives a better hookset, too.

SUMMER
Rating: 10

Fishing is tough in the summer. Conditions are not favorable because of the heat and pleasure boaters. The hot water can make fish lethargic. One way to beat this is to get deep. Deep fish are more stable. Deep crappie can adjust to difficult conditions.

Summer stumps can be in 8 feet of water or as deep as 25 feet. The rule of thumb is: early summer 8-15 feet; early midsummer 12-22 feet; and late midsummer is 10-15 feet if the lake has a thermocline, deeper if it doesn't.

Techniques can be whatever a fisherman wants to use. The edges of mid-depth stumps can be trolled. Deep, tight fish

Stumps, Snags & Logs

A. Deep Stump: perfect spot for winter and summer crappie. Vertical techniques would be the most efficient for fishing this stump.

B. Snags: deep to mid depth water, cover from top to bottom; excellent for year-round crappie catching. Fish these snags using your favorite technique.

C. Sunken Log: good depth for crappie. Casting, vertical jigging, and slip-float rigs would all be good tactics for this log.

D. Shallow Snags: primarily a spring and fall spot. Casting or jigging.

Seasonal Structure 110

Chatt Martin using a popular springtime technique:
jigging shallow wood structure.
Muddy water lets him get very close to the fish without spooking them.

can be caught by vertical jigging.

Baits don't have to be left as long in the summer as in the winter. Crappie will usually take them if they want the bait. The exception to this is in the dogdays of summer when the water is very hot.

Minnows are good summer baits but jigs can work too. Match the bait to the presentation and then adjust as needed.

FALL
Rating: 7

This is a great time because the fish are active and moving. An isolated stump on a point is a spot just waiting for a fall crappie. Another place is a line of stumps or snags. Crappie/wood combinations can't be beat in this season; just as in other seasons.

A free-fall jig or a jig/float combo are good in the fall. Fast trolling is another good tactic. Trolling lets you present a lot of baits to a lot of fish. Isolated or numbers of stumps and logs on a flat is an ideal place to check. Crappie may be on the stumps or scattered between them.

Fast retrieves (fast for crappie) is fine in the fall. Curly tails and spinner baits are good for all depths and areas.

FACTORS
Stumps, Snags and Logs

***Wind** -can be an advantage fishing shallow stumps; a disadvantage fishing deep.
***Strong Cold Front** -not good, but an advantage because it will put fish tighter to cover.
***Clouds/Rain** -usually no major problem.
***Sun** -puts fish tight to shallow cover or sends them deep.
***Fast Rise/Fall** -must test-fish to find their depth.
***Mud** -if consistent with other lake water, good in the shallows.
***High Water** -Usually good depending upon the season and depths.

Chapter 11

Fallen Trees
(Laydowns)

There are few structures better than a fallen tree. A tree downed in the water offers practically everything a crappie could want.

The depth range depends upon the height of the tree and the depth of the water near shoreline. A good fallen tree, also called a laydown, will typically be in 10 to 20 feet of water at the top end.

Where are laydowns found? Any shoreline where trees are present. Laydowns are more prevalent along banks that wash with current and/or waves.

Why fish? A treetop, small jon boat, cane pole and a straw hat is the picture people have etched in their minds of a 'crappie fisherman'. There's nothing wrong with that picture. It was the simple, efficient way to catch fish. Today things have changed, but the treetops are still a favorite hangout of crappie and will continue to be for generations to come.

A fallen tree is perfect wood cover. It offers shade, cover for protection, habitat for baitfish and is a good all-around home.

Locating a laydown can be obvious. Limbs are sticking up everywhere in and above the water. Knowing where to fish is simple.

Other laydowns are not so obvious. A tree may have all or most of its top below water. This one can be a little tricky to find, but an experienced fisherman will spot the signs.

The third possibility is that a tree is completely under water. Luck and a locator is the way to find submerged tops, unless there are indicators on the bank.

Bank signs may include a large trunk on the bank entering the water. This one is an easy find. It shows the presence of a fallen tree, the angle gives an approximate depth, and the direction shows how the tree is positioned. It doesn't get any easier.

Other tree trunks may be partially visible on shore and/or where they enter the water. Moving close to the bank gives a better view of the size, direction and other details.

Rootwads are another good indicator of a laydown. A root system may be under the water, in the edge of the water or high on a bank. The underwater rootwad is best because it means that fewer fishermen will find it. Also, fish can use all portions of a completely submerged tree.

Therefore, a fallen tree has three main sections that can be visually spotted. These are the top (limbs and branches), trunk and roots. Searching for these can be a good way to find excellent fishing.

SPRING
Rating: 10
My dad has tied to many treetops and loaded his small

but any season can be productive. Tops have been and will continue to be great crappie structures.

A long pole with a minnow under a slip-float is a good technique. This rig is the modern version of the cane pole.

The newer poles are extendible fiberglass models. They are commonly referred to as 'zip' poles because they can be quickly transformed from a small package into a fully-extended long pole. The sliding sections zip into place. These poles are simple with no reels or line guides. They are inexpensive and rugged. Also, they are a good weapon for catching fish from the branches and limbs of a fallen tree.

Another long pole method is tightlining a jig. This has many names including doodle-sockin', dipping, and jigging. The tightline technique is best performed by upgrading to a quality graphite pole. More bites will be felt and more fish caught.

Line is an important factor when tightlining. The new superlines are tough and thin. They can be an advantage, especially when fishing clear water.

Another good line that many experts prefer is high visibility line. Visible line shows where it's located in the water, side movements when a crappie is running, and even small 'tic-tic' bites before they are felt. Visible line is a good choice for line watching while longpoling.

The proper presentation is important when fishing a laydown that's full of small limbs. A straight up and down presentation is important. Working through the limbs is generally not a problem when care is used when raising the bait.

A bait should be placed in every opening where a bait can be dropped. Don't rush a bait. Fish each spot thoroughly. Crappie may be along the main trunk, within the thickest limbs,

Seasonal Structure 116

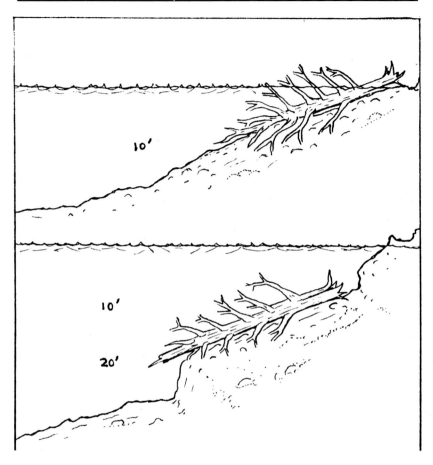

Laydowns

(top) Tree with top in 10 feet of water. Limbs are sticking in plain view (a calling card for crappie fishermen). Roots easy to see. The best season for you to fish this laydown is spring; followed by fall and then summer.

(bottom) Tree in depths ranging from 5 feet down to 20. All of the tree is submerged and fishable. It's not in plain view for all to see. It's associated with a good drop-off. This submerged tree gets an A+ rating for all seasons. (Don't even tell your friends about this one).

staged just above the limbs, or holding on the outside edges of the wood. There are plenty of places to fish in a fallen tree.

FALL
Rating: 8

Fall is very similar to spring when fishing laydowns. Fall rates an 8 because crappie enjoy actively feeding as water temperatures become more pleasant. Trees in the water provide a home for these crappie.

Techniques are generally the same as in the spring. However, there is one important difference in the fall. Hit-and-run tactics are better in the fall while spring requires more patience in one spot.

A tightlined minnow or jig on a graphite pole is best for quickly probing a laydown. The graphite gives the advantage of better feel to detect bumps with cover and light bites from crappie.

A small jig should be dropped into a potential area then held motionless. Small vibrations from the pole along with body movements will give the jig plenty of action on the long pole. After a count of "five", drop the bait about a foot and count again. The last move is a very slow rise about two feet followed by another count. If not bit, lift the jig and place it in another hole in the top.

A jig/minnow combo is an excellent bait for dippin'. The jig weight keeps the minnow from roaming and wrapping around a limb. Yet, the action of the minnow and the attraction of the jig colors will draw the attention of any nearby crappie.

A 1/8 ounce jig head is great for going straight up and down in limbs. The weight and bigger hook also makes it easier to shake loose if hung.

SUMMER
Rating: 6

The rating in summer can vary tremendously from lake to lake. Extreme temperature, too much boat traffic, and other factors will influence crappie moods and may even run them out of a top onto a deeper channel.

The good news is that disturbances don't always mean that a fallen tree is bad in the summer. My partner and I fished a midsummer club tournament and probably caught 150 fish from one old, fallen tree trunk. It was positioned on a sloped, natural rocky bank that quickly turned to mud. Due to age, little remains of the old tree except for the primary trunk and a couple of limbs. This wasn't a spot that you would be expect to hold numbers of midsummer crappie...but it did.

The moral to the above example is: locations must be tested by fishing. Don't spend an hour on a tree that isn't producing, but don't just look at one and say, "I can tell by looking that it doesn't have fish on it."

The typical up and down vertical techniques described in the spring and fall sections still apply. One other tactic should also be mentioned for this season. It's the minnow and float. Basics include a fallen tree with age (only major limbs still attached), anchored boat and casting outfits.

Here's how to do it. Anchor by referencing to the position of the tree, wind and current. Be in a position where baits are carried to the tree, not toward the boat. This keeps lines tight making placement easier. It also allows a quicker hook set and baits remain in the strike zone instead of drifting out to the boat.

Use two or three poles. This number is easy to watch and control while improving chances of more bites. A minnow under a float will do all the work while you relax.

Fallen Tree

This old, washed-out tree is in a good location to hold crappie. It's on an outside bend (which is why it got the dirt washed out from under the roots) and is situated on a contour change. Rootwads and tree trunks are tell-tale signs of better things down below.

Look at the water depth and angle of the trunk to determine how far into the water the top is likely to be. The best fishing may be 30-40 feet from where the tree enters the water.

WINTER
Rating: 5

Fallen trees in shallow water gets a "0". Laydowns extending into deeper water on steep banks get a "10". This is because water temperatures and depth are very critical during the cold months.

This section will detail fallen trees in water that's deep enough for winter crappie. These depths include 15 to 20 feet in a normal stained-water reservoir.

Techniques are the same as the other seasons with one exception: weights should be increased when fishing deep water in and around wood.

Vertical tightlining techniques are the ideal choice. Either minnow, jigs or combinations can be used. Minnows should be fished with sinkers close to the hooks. The sinker should be in the 1/4 to 1/2 ounce range This will prevent the minnow from swimming around limbs and twigs.

A 1/16 ounce jig can be used if everything is perfectly still. Jigs should be 1/8 ounce when any current or wind is present. You may even want to add a split-shot if the conditions are bad. It's important that the jig is under the rod tip, not drifting sideways.

A winter crappie often needs plenty of time. I don't know why they sometimes take so long to bite. One group of fishermen believe that crappie are comparing the bait to the amount of energy they have to expend to eat it. Others believe they are just more finicky. Some say it's because they can see the bait better. It could be that they just don't eat often and are in a negative feeding mood most of the time. I personally don't know why fish are slow to bite, but I know that a certain percentage of the fish will bite if a bait is put in front of their nose.

Crappie compare somewhat to other creatures when feeding. For example, even when you're not hungry, what happens when your favorite dessert is placed in front of you? Most of the time you'll eat it. The same is true with crappie. If a minnow or inviting jig is placed in front of a crappie's nose, he'll probably eat it. It may take him a minute or two to decide...so leave it in front of him awhile when winter fishing.

FACTORS
Fallen Trees

*****Wind** -no problem.
*****Strong Cold Fronts** -fish get tight into the cover and may get lockjaw.
*****Clouds/Rain** -fish may move higher into the cover and also move to the outside edges.
*****Sun** -deeper and tighter to cover and also move to the outside edges.
*****Fast Rise/Fall** -will probably stay in the top but change depths and maybe position.
*****Current** -crappie will get on the backside of the cover for a current break.
*****High Water** -will stay but position themselves in a comfort zone based upon water conditions and temperatures.
*****Fishing Pressure** -visible laydowns are a magnet to fish and fishermen. Exposed trees will get a lot of fishing pressure. Smaller average size fish is the result.

Seasonal Structure 122

Sam Heaton

More on Fallen Trees
Subject Expert: Sam Heaton

Sam Heaton has guided for many years on Alabama's Weiss Lake. He is in big demand as a seminar speaker and products promoter. Heaton has tips to share about his experiences fishing fallen trees.

The first requirement is a good depth range. The end of the laydown must be in at least 10 feet of water. If it has ten or more feet of water, fish will stay there and work up and down the tree.

The biggest fear a crappie has is predation from above. Predator fish, birds and even man are likely to attack from above. Crappie become spooky in shallow water.

What type tree do you want?

I like to see a tree that's been dead a long time before it falls in the water. Insects are in it. The sap that produces acidity is gone. I also like a lot of limb structure like a hickory or oak.

Techniques and equipment?

I fish from the shallow layer of water to the deep, especially in the spring.

I'm going to fish a B&M graphite jig pole straight up and down with a tube jig. The tubes are good baits and easy to use. I always pull the knot back to keep my jig horizontal.

Presentations are always as still as I can possibly make them. There's no way I can hold the tube jig still enough for the jig not to move and swim around.

The next way I'll fish it is with a slip-cork and minnow. Again, I'm going straight up and down. I can control the minnow.

When fishing live bait in a brush pile, the closer you put that bait to a hook, the less movement the minnow is going to have. If the brush is really thick and congested, I'm going to have that weight slide right down on my hook. The minnow can't swim around. If I'm in open water, I want the sinker a foot or more above the bait.

I always hook minnows through the eyes. They will live longer, pull behind the hook, not get curly, and they won't see what's fixin' to happen to them.

Jigging and slip-corking are year-round methods.

Tip?

I rig my line to be as long as my pole no matter what depth I'm fishing. I may switch from a 14 foot pole to a 10 foot or vice versa. When I catch a fish, I want to be able to swing him right into my hand.

Final comments about laydowns?

Let's cut to the chase....fishing visible cover is the easiest method I can teach a person to do. Why? The only thing he has to have is a small jon boat, boat paddle, fiberglass pole and a good graphite pole to thoroughly fish a laydown. That's all the basics necessary. No special depthfinders, trolling motors, and the special equipment everyone thinks you have to have.

It's natural. It's the old cane pole method with better equipment.

Section 4
Natural Structures

-Points
-Deep & Mid Depth Weeds
-Rock Bluffs
-Flats
    -Shallow
    -Mid Depth
    -Deep
-Humps & Underwater Islands
-High Water Structure

Chapter 12

Points

Points are runways for crappie. Temperature, light penetration and other factors determine when, where and how crappie use points.

Fishing this structure is relatively easy. The most difficult part is keeping track of the movements of crappie from day to day. Also, severe wind can hinder fishing in open water.

Points can be long or short, narrow or wide and deep or shallow. They may have a mud, rock or gravel bottom. They may be bare or chocked-full of cover. Therefore, points are independent of one another. Each has its own characteristics that make it a good or bad seasonal structure. Fishing experience at points will let you learn which ones in your home waters are best.

Points can be any depth. Match the depths with the season when searching for points.

Where found? They are everywhere in a typical lake or river. Points may be long or they may be very subtle.

Locating points can be done with a topographical map. They are easy to find. By picking the ones in the seasonal depth zone, many can be eliminated.

Points are also easy to find visually. Looking at the bank gives exact locations. Slopes and depths can usually be estimated from the bank.

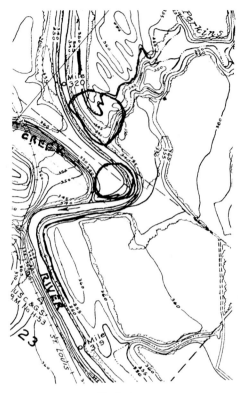

Points

(top) A long, sloping point dropping into a major channel. The river channel side is a good winter spot. The shallow side going into the creek is excellent during a quick warm-up in the winter or spring.

(bottom) This point is long and flat, then drops suddenly into deep water. The topo map doesn't show, but this entire point is very shallow and stump filled. It's a hit & miss spot, but can be loaded with fish when conditions are right. The channel edge may have fish any time of year.

SPRING
Rating: 7

Points are another structure you can add to your arsenal of places to catch fish. An interesting thing about points is that the numbers of concentrated fish may be less than on other structures. However, when scattered cover is present, a point may provide hours of fair to good action.

Another interesting fact is that fish often move up and down a point. Spring fish are moving but throw in sunlight, clouds and shifting winds and fish will change depths several times a day. Temperature and light penetration are key elements. Find the right depths and you'll likely find a gold mine of crappie.

Spring techniques can vary. Two totally different yet proven tactics include the use of floats. The first is a jig and float. This rig keeps the bait at a constant depth. It's excellent when fish are scattered across a point. Fan casting a jig and float is easy because the rig can be stopped, pulled and let drift with the wind and current.

Jig speed should be as fast as crappie allows it to be. What this means is that a moderate speed is used to start. If crappie are caught, the jig is pulled faster until the crappie no longer hit. Then, slow the jig back down. This tactic allows you to work more water. Also, when no fish are caught at a medium speed the bait can be slowed down and occasionally stopped.

The second technique is a slip-float and minnow. This technique is usually best from an anchored boat. The presentation is much slower than with the jig and float. It gives crappie a chance to see a bait for a long time.

The slip-float rigs can be cast a long distance so you can stay away from the fish and not spook them. The baits are slowly moved along over cover making it the same as an

Seasonal Structure   130

This is a small but potentially good point.
The gravel adds to it's attractiveness. Small points like this are easy to find, quick to check and simple to fish.

extremely slow drift. It's a good, relaxing way to fish. Using two or three rigs allows you to scan an area and work it thoroughly.

A third presentation option is to use one or two minnow rigs and cast a jig and float. This gives a one-two punch with varied baits and speeds.

WINTER
Rating: 7

Winter points are good but different than in the other seasons. They are points that have steep drop-offs and are located near or against a channel.

Techniques include casting a free-fall jig from an anchored boat. This may be a challenge in deep water, but has proven to be a dynamite presentation.

Jigs rank high in the winter. Casting a 1/16 ounce jig gives a moderate fall and lets the jig be retrieved slowly without hugging to the bottom unless it's barely crawled. A 1/8 ounce is best when the wind, waves and very deep water are present.

Probably the most popular technique is tightlining. This lets bait depth be set or changed while boat control directs the baits into specific areas of the point.

Vertical jigging can be with jigs or minnows. It's a good idea to give crappie both options to see which they prefer.

Another vertical option is to use a drop-loop and minnow on top and a heavy jig on bottom. A 1/8 Google-Eye jig or a 1/4 ounce round head with a tube are examples of jigs for jig/minnow combos. This gives crappie two different baits while using the jig for additional rig weight.

FALL
Rating: 6

Mid depth and shallow points can be good in the fall. Gradual slopes and scattered stumps are typical fall cover. Points are natural places for shad to be located; crappie will be nearby relating to stumps. Be aggressive in the fall. Techniques are similar to the spring when areas are fished fast until fish are found.

Baits need to be aggressive too. Tube jigs are fine, but

POINT & LAYDOWN....THE DEADLY COMBINATION
These fishermen are working a large, deep point. Notice the huge rootwad at the shoreline and the tree extending far out into the deep water. This structure is good for many species of fish, especially crappie.

curly tails and Creek Runners are very good when searching for active fish.

One exception to being aggressive is when a front or water condition slow the crappie. When the fish slow down, so should retrieve speeds. Make adjustments to the situation. Deeper water may also be something to look for during tough fishing conditions.

SUMMER
Rating: 5

Long points extending into deep water rate a 5 in the summer. These points provide comfort zones. They are very good when they contact a deep channel.

Presentations are no secret. Typical summer presentations and speeds will work.

FACTORS
Points

***Wind** -not a problem unless too strong to fish.
***Strong Cold Front** -fish will be negative and usually go deeper.
***Clouds/Rain** -makes trolling excellent for finding and catching random fish.
***Sun** -fish move deeper.
***Current** -too strong will run them to other locations.
***High Water** -ok.

Chapter 13

Deep & Mid Depth Weeds

Deep weeds are productive hotspots. They are unique because of the type of water they grow in. Catching fish requires knowing how crappie relate to the weeds and the never-ending changes taking place in and around weedbeds.

Weeds are in all water; deep weeds are not. Deep weeds are usually found in lakes with very clear water. Light penetration makes deep growth possible (muddy water doesn't). Natural and some manmade lakes are known for their good clearwater fishing around weeds.

Why fish? Because a patch of weeds is a serious fish attractor. Weeds are extremely important for catching fish in waters where they are present.

Locating deep and mid depth weeds may take some time. They aren't shown on a map. The first recommendation I can make is to check with local experts. A guide, marina operator or local fisherman will be able to tell you if weeds are present, their depth and some general areas to start your search.

Any serious search requires a locator. It reveals depth, bottom hardness, weeds and fish. The most important information is the depth and weeds. Finding weeds, determining their height and identifying the maximum depth at which they grow will play a role in fishing strategies.

Finding weeds is much easier than finding a piece of isolated cover like a brush pile or stump. Weeds can be found by checking points, humps and any other structure with long, sloping contours.

To diagnose a weedy area, start shallow to ensure that weeds are present. If you spot them in 8 to 10 feet, ease deeper until they disappear on the locator. You will learn several key elements: presence of weeds; maximum depth of weeds; how tall the weeds are at different depths; and the density of the weeds. With this information, logical fishing begins.

WINTER
Rating: 10

Weeds in 10 feet of water and deeper are excellent structures. Fish like to use them for all their daily activities: feeding, as a reference when traveling and for hiding from predators. The job of the fisherman is to diagnosis the weeds and determine the crappie's pattern for the day.

A good technique for weeds is trolling. It's an excellent way to become familiar with the weeds, learn a pattern and catch fish.

Here's an example. The weeds extend from the shoreline into 20 feet of water. Those at 15 feet are 4 feet tall. You should make a trolling run over water 15-16 feet deep. The baits are kept at depths of 6-10 feet, or just above the weeds. A long run will indicate if fish are present and active at those depths.

Weeds can be a fustration. However, crappie use them for a home and feeding ground so you should prepare yourself mentally and with the techniques to give you an edge for catching fish from this type structure.

The locator will also show anything 'different' in the weed pattern that might be a clue to a hotspot.

A second trolling run is made at 18-20 feet. This will show if fish are present on the deepest, outside fringes of the weeds.

A third run at 12-13 feet will complete the check for a pattern on the weeds. After this run, repeat trolling at the best depths.

Top trolling baits in the weeds include a 1/32 or 1/16 ounce jig. Different types and colors should be tested. (White is a good clear water color). Trolling speeds will control the bait depths and action.

A second method for catching weedline crappie is casting. The area should first be diagnosed by trolling as previously described. Key areas are noted. Good spots include points, small drop-offs, and irregularities in the weeds.

Casting is targeted specifically to marked locations (casting is not a good search technique). Casting allows good control of the bait so weeds can be carefully worked.

SPRING
Rating: 7

Late spring is when most lakes see crappie heading to the weeds. Before that, spawning takes priority with weeds being a moderate factor.

FALL/WINTER
Rating: 3

Deep weeds can be an important cover, but most of the time they are minor. They are on the downswing with decaying. Decaying weeds are the worst do to bad pH and oxygen during the period. After that, the remaining dead matter is a mediocre cover.

Tactics and presentations are the same as other seasons.

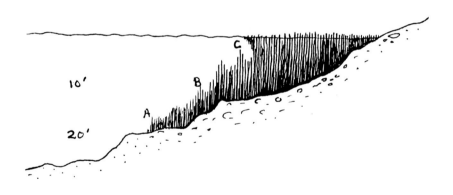

Deep Weeds
A. Excellent in post-spawn, summer and early fall.
   Techniques: deep jigging or slow trolling.
B. Good spring, summer and fall.
   Slip-float, casting, or trolling.
C. Best in spring and fall.
   Casting jig or minnow under a float.

Seasonal Structure

FACTORS
Deep & Mid Depth Weeds

***Wind** -annoying to fishing but seldom bothers fish.

***Conditions** -Water temperature, sunlight and the shade of the weeds cause crappie to move a lot. Checking different depths is the best way to learn what fish are doing.

***pH** -seasonal changes bring about different stages of weed development or deterioration. The pH level is very important. If you're serious about fishing weeds, check the area with a Combo-C-Lector pH probe to find the most productive depth zone.

Chapter 14

Rock Bluffs

Bluffs are different than most other structures. They can be intimidating. However, a little practice can help you gain confidence in these tall, rocky structures.

The practical depth range in muddy water is 0-25 feet; stained 0-35; and clear 10-50.

Bluffs are very common on deep lakes in the hills and mountains. Bluffs can be found on many rivers and reservoirs.

Why fish this structure? Crappie want comfort, food and safety. Bluffs can fulfill these requirements. For example, comfort and safety are available because of the different depths. The depths combine with hiding places in the rocks to provide a getaway when attackers are near.

Food is available because of the rocks. Wood cover in the area enhances the spot as a feeding ground. Minnows, crayfish, and other stay meals are common along a bluff. Fishermen can take advantage of the opportunity to take feeding bluff crappie when they're present.

Locating bluffs doesn't take a rocket scientist. A topo map will readily show them. Tight contour lines are easy to see on a map. Visual inspections are another way to find bluffs. Unlike underwater cover and ledges, bluffs are easy to find and fish.

SUMMER
Rating: 7

Bluffs are good to try in the summer. Deep water is available and fish can be found on a locator.

Fishing a bluff is a mix of simplicity and problems. The best method is vertical jigging or slow trolling. It's a simple method of fishing. The problems are sinker-eating rocks and keeping baits deep.

You should concentrate on depths based upon locator

indications. Fish showing at 30 feet don't need baits at 12 or 16 feet....daahhh. Baits should be at 27 to 30 feet. Sounds simple, but many fishermen fail to adjust to the fish. Baits are often fished outside of the strike zone. Watch your locator....put baits on the crappie's heads. It's easy to do when fishing a bluff.

Chatt Martin....On The Rocks.
Chatt has great success on rip-rap, bluffs, and natural rock/mud edges.
Rocks are a key element that's never ignored when he's establishing a pattern.

WINTER
Rating: 6

A difficult rating because of the variations of lakes and fish movements. Winter crappie want deep water to be available. Bluffs offer deep water and usually other features that crappie want.

Winter fishing is the same as summer. The primary change might be the baits. Winter is a good time to fish jigs. Also, downsizing can trigger extra bites.

FALL
Rating: 4

Fall fish are on the move. Expect them to be 8-12 feet in most slight to moderately stained waters. Tactics remain the same but casting can be added because of the shallower depths.

SPRING
Rating: 4

Fish move relatively shallow in the spring. The primary reason to check a bluff is to look at the bottom where big rocks

---

FACTORS
Rock Bluffs

***Wind** -little or no problem unless the bluff is directly in the wind.
***Front** -ok; fish can move to a different level.
***Clouds/Rain** -ok.
***Sun** -fish deep.
***Current** -bad.
***Fishing Pressure** -usually not a problem.

turn to gravel and then to mud. If the bottom isn't too deep, big slabs may spawn on the deep gravel bottom at 15-25 feet. It's a long shot, but one that can pay big returns.

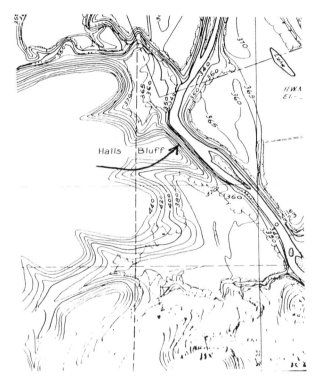

Bluff
Notice the tight contour lines on
the bank that lead right on down into the water.
A straight up-and-down bank is the result.

MORE ON BLUFFS
Subject Experts: Tim Martin; Chatt Martin

Tim and Chatt Martin are brothers, crappie seminar speakers, and tournament fishermen. They are familiar with bluffs and are glad to share their knowledge.

Chatt immediately started drawing to explain typical bluff features. *Bluffs are places where you can fish a lot of different depths at the same time. The areas marked with a (1) are primary places to fish. They're important because of the different depths including a slope or becoming a small flat. The distance (3) may be a hundred yards or a mile; it doesn't matter. The triangles at the end will be the best fishing.*

Chatt continues, *One thing we like to do is fish one of the triangles (1) and then slow troll to the other thru zone (2). This may be a transition area. Any cover will definitely hold fish.*

Tim jumps in with some tips. *Rock slides (4) are another excellent place to fish. If you look up on the rocks and there's a big hunk that's out of the bluff, then there's a rock slide underneath.*

"A vertical bluff can be made great by suspending a brush pile from a rope. Rope and weight the brush pile, then tie it up on the bank. All of a sudden the fish have something that will stop them. I do this and it works. I like to hide my lines and ropes supporting the tree so other fishermen will have trouble finding it.

Another good place to fish is where you have a long bluff and then mud. That's a transition area. That's a spot we'll go check.

Chatt says, *Bluffs may be straight up and down or stair-stepped. I like the stair-step bluffs because then we have something that will hold fish at different levels. A bluff going from 0-60 feet is tough to fish.*

Seasonally, a bluff will probably be better in the summer, fall, and winter.

Tactics? *When temperatures are below 50 degrees,* says Chatt, *leave the minnows at the bait shop. I want a 1/4 ounce jig to fish deep on a bluff. I usually deadstick because I can't hold it still enough.*

Equipment? *A 7 foot medium action Quantum rod, 6 lb. test Fireline and a Crappie-Finder Zebco reel.*

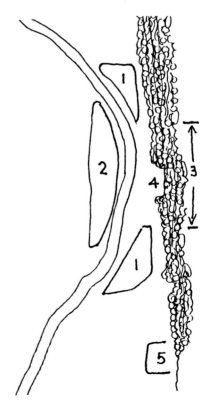

Bluff
1. Primary spots where the river channel swings into and away from bluff.
2. Transition area. Sometimes used by crappie to go from one bluff area to another.
3. Distance between prime locations.
4. Rock slide. Any major indentions in a bluff may have been caused by a slide; part of the bluff slid into the lake. This means that rock and irregular features are underwater.
5. Rock/mud bank transition spot; always a spot worth fishing.

Chapter 15

Shallow Flats

FLATS

The next three chapters discuss three distinct flats: shallow, mid depth and deep. Each one has similarities but seasonal conditions make them different.

A flat is an area that's flat in comparison to the surrounding terrain. For example, it's a farmer's field in a meadow surrounded by hills. The field may have a slight slope, but it's relatively flat.

Lakes, rivers, and reservoirs usually have many flats that once were fields. Other flats may be the tops of a ledge next to a creek or river channel. They may be the site of a home place covered with water after a dam was built. There are many reasons for flats and there are many reasons why you should be interested in them for catching fish.

Why fish a flat? A flat is often a feeding ground for crappie. They can move onto a flat, feed and return to safer water.

A flat is a resting place. A prime example is the period immediately following the spawn. Post-spawn crappie are widely known for suspending in flats.

Flats can be at any depth so they are seasonally good structures. Are they perfect? Definitely not. But they are productive during different phases and should not be overlooked.

Locating a flat isn't too difficult. A contour (topo) map is the easiest way. Areas with few contour lines are the flats. A locator will confirm a flat. Notice that fish in very shallow water are seldom shown due to the tiny cone angle and because the boat spooks the shallow fish.

SHALLOW FLATS

SPRING
Rating: 7

Shallow water and springtime go together no matter which structure we discuss. A flat in shallow water is best during spawn and post-spawn. Depths are 1-6 feet in stained water.

Drifting, fast trolling or casting is the way to pursue shallow spring crappie scattered on a flat. Drifting is relaxing. Baits under floats can be kept a long distance behind the boat so fish won't be spooked.

Fast trolling is good too, but long poles (14-20 feet) are needed to keep baits away from the boat. Fish on each side will be the crappie that bite best.

Casting is a third technique for crappie on a shallow flat. Casting should only be done in areas where crappie have been found. Drifting and trolling are much better search methods than casting. The casting advantage is to target a specific

151 *Shallow Flats*

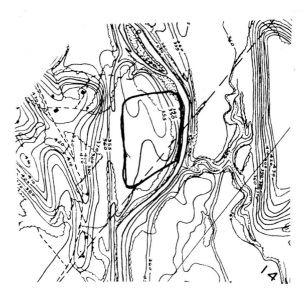

Shallow Flat
A contour map (and lower unit on motor) are good ways to find shallow flats. Circled is a flat; noted with contour lines far apart.

area and keep getting a bait to the fish without going over them with a boat.

Baits can include both minnows and jigs. Drifting is the best method for minnows. Casting and trolling are the best methods for using artificial.

WINTER
Rating: 7

So you think I've gone bonkers with this rating? Most of the time, winter shallow flats are zero. The water is too cold and shallow for any fish.

Give a shallow flat two days of sunshine and warm southerly breezes. Shad will move up into the shallowest water to enjoy the warmth. Crappie are soon to follow. When crappie are up in the shallow flats in winter and late winter, the rating is a 10-plus. It can be the fastest action of the year.

Fishing shallow flats is a hit-and-miss proposition. A fisherman should check very shallow water at different times throughout the day. If there is no action, leave it alone. If a crappie is caught, chances are excellent that many more fish will be with him.

Casting is the method of choice. A jig under a float will let the bait be worked very slow or fast. A good technique is to crank slow for 3 to 6 seconds and then stop the baits for about 3 seconds.

Another way to cast is from an anchored boat. Cast out three poles each rigged with a float and minnow. This is a good way to catch scattered fish or to concentrate several baits into one area.

FALL
Rating: 5

Fall crappie will go shallow to feed. They like areas with some cover. Stumps, an old fence or a secondary drop will hold them in an area that has baitfish. Fishing tactics are similar to winter with one exception; a spinner is often a good bait if the fish are active.

This crappie pair was taken from a shallow mud flat just off of a river channel bend.

SUMMER
Rating: 3

Flats less than 5 or 6 feet are not playgrounds for summer crappie. The best way to fish shallow flats is to spot check them by fancasting. A fisherman may get lucky and find crappie. If none are quickly found, head back toward deeper water.

**FACTORS
Shallow Flats**

***Wind** -can be an advantage for getting close to the fish.
***Front** -bad.
***Clouds/Rain** -good; fish less spooky.
***Sun** -ok.
***Mud** -good in cold water because it warms quickly.
***Current** -bad.
***Fishing Pressure** -can be a problem if other fishermen see you catching fish.
***Boat Traffic** -a very big problem when fishing shallow.

Chapter 16

Mid Depth Flats

Mid depth flats can be considered those areas in 5-15 feet of water in a typical stained lake. Clear water mid depth flats may range from 10-25 feet deep.

Mid flats are often beside river or creek channels. They can be in a main lake or in the back of a creek. The flat has excellent potential if the channel ledge is in about 15 feet of water and breaks into an immediate flat.

Why fish? Because mid-depths are in the crappie comfort zone during much of the year. Another advantage is that baitfish like the same zone and are often found roaming the flats.

Cover can be natural or manmade. Cover of some type should definitely be available.

Mid depth flats are easy to fish. Almost any technique will work.

The easiest way to find a mid depth flat is with a map. As previously discussed, contour lines far apart indicate a flat area. A fisherman can pinpoint flats at the proper depth with good associated structures nearby. A locator will confirm the right areas.

SPRING

Rating: 7

There are two times that mid depth flats are particularly appealing. The first is in late winter and very early spring. That's when fish are actively feeding and on the move. They are gorging themselves preparing for the spawn. Surface temperatures will be in the low to upper 50's. Crappie may be at any depth within the mid depth zone.

The second time for outstanding fishing on mid depth flats is the post-spawn period. Fish are stressed out from spawning so they'll go out to these flats and rest. They will usually suspend off the bottom. They'll stay there while recuperating. They'll be in a very negative feeding mood; they don't want to eat. However, post-spawn crappie are difficult and there are few places better than a mid depth flat to search.

The best way to catch fish is to present baits to a lot of fish and hope a few are triggered into reaction or feeding bites. Specific techniques include drifting, pulling and trolling.

The advantage of drifting is that the baits will be moving with the boat. The boat speed can be adjusted as current and wind moves it along. Drifting will be over the same depth of water, so baits can be set and not have to be readjusted constantly.

Trolling and pulling have the same concept as drifting, except more precise boat control is maintained. All methods put multiple baits in front of a lot of fish. Speeds should be constant and at a reasonable speed.

(right) Steve McCadams and Jim Perry are Kentucky Lake guides and the 1996 Crappiethon Classic Champions. They fish different patterns depending upon crappie movements. One of their best spring and fall patterns is driven stakebeds in shallow and mid depth flats.

SUMMER
Rating: 8

Summer crappie are similar to spring fish except they can be more aggressive, especially in early summer. They'll be at the lowest range of the mid depths. That makes them more stable so it's an advantage to have them deeper.

Summer techniques are the same as in the spring. Trolling, pulling and drifting are all good methods.

Baits can be more aggressive in the summer. Curly tail jigs, minnow-shaped jigs and large Umbrella tubes are all good choices. Jig weights must be the correct size to stay at the right depths.

Seasonal Structure 158

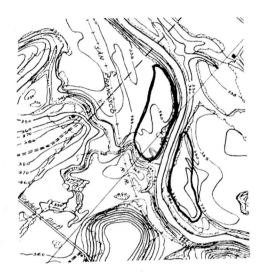

Mid Depth Flat
This topo map indicates a 10-foot flat (circled area). Use a map to find flats at the depth you want.

FALL
Rating: 7

Fall mid depth flats are good because fish are going back and forth from deep water to shallow. They are actively feeding, so finding crappie on a mid depth flat is an opportunity for a fisherman to catch a lot of fish.

Fall tactics can be the same as the spring and summer. Casting is also good in the fall when fish are patterned to a particular depth. Repeated casts allows you to really invade a crappie's hangout.

WINTER
Rating: 7

Winter mid depth flats may be a 1 or 10. The lower depths are not bad during some of the winter period. When fish are present, they rate a 10 because crappie are active.

Winter fish often stay deeper than the mid depths and they also like to hold very close to drops. This can make flats a zero. Spot-check an area and then decide whether to fish them or move to another structure.

Techniques should be slower than in other seasons. Any vertical presentation is a good choice. Minnows should be included in the arsenal of baits. The natural thing is often best. Jigs work too but must be weighted to stay deep even when moving.

FACTORS
Mid Depth Flats

*****Front** -not good; severity depends upon many combinations of factors.
*****Sun/Clouds/Rain** -ok, but fish may change depths.
*****Current** -strong current is very bad.
*****High Water** -ok.

Seasonal Structure

Chapter 17

Deep Flats

Deep (in stained waters) is anything below 15 feet. Flats in these depths are usually near primary river channels. Deep flats often have a lot of silting causing them to be soft. Primary cover will be drifted logs, manmade cover and sometimes natural wood.

Why fish a deep flat? Deep water periods are the time for you to get baits down to the fish. There's not always structure available for fish, so deep flats are a place they can go. Deep flats are not popular with most fishermen, but since crappie may locate on them, so should you.

Locating deep flats is similar to finding them during the other seasons: a map and locator.

Seasonal Structure 162

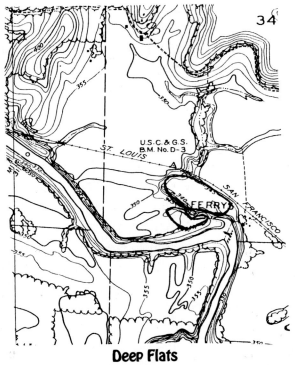

Deep Flats
Even on this Corps of Engineers lake that has a 6 foot deep average over-all depth, there are a few deep flats available to fish. The ones circled are 15-20 feet deep. Most lakes will have deeper flats that you may choose.

SUMMER
Rating: 7

Summer is the time for many crappie to go deep. Early to mid summer will be the best periods. Late summer will be good if no thermocline sets up.

Techniques for summer can be any method that gets a bait down to the proper depth. The number one all-around technique has to be slow trolling. This tactic lets a fisherman put three or four poles (where legal) over the side of the boat. A controlled boat against the wind makes slow presentations easy. The fisherman can stop and stay when good cover or concentrations of fish are found.

Baits for deep slow trolling include minnows on a Kentucky Lake style rig. When presented slow, minnows are difficult to beat. If jigs are preferred, 1/32 ounce jigs can be substituted for minnows on the same rig. Or, a 1/16 or 1/8 ounce jig with a large split-shot can be used.

Pulling is another tactic that is good for deep flats. Pulling is a sideways drift of the boat with the wind. The purpose is to stay at a specific depth range and cover a wide path with the baits triggering active fish.

Pulling gets multiple baits down to the bottom and keeps them there. Deep pulling rigs consist of two 1/8 ounce jigs. Once the boat is drifting at fishing speed, baits are lowered until they touch bottom and then they are reeled up tow or three cranks.

Like most other structures, seasons and situations, it's time to change structures when no fish are found in thirty or forty minutes.

WINTER
Rating: 7

Winter is another time when fish are likely to be found on a deep flat. More important than in any other season, good structure must be present. Crappie won't meander all day on a bare flat when a drop-off with cover is nearby. However, good manmade or natural cover dramatically changes your chances for success and makes the flat a legitimate structure opportunity.

Tactics, baits and presentations are similar to summer deep flats. The only addition is casting a free-fall jig. Casting from an anchored boat is a good way to fish when fish are marked and pinpointed to a particular brush pile or set of stumps.

SPRING
Rating: 3

Deep flats are fair to good during two situations in the spring. One, when the water is still too cold for the spawn migration. Two, during bad weather and water conditions. Barometric pressure or bad water may put them into the deep waters.

Deep flats in the spring are primarily structures to be used during bad weather/water conditions.

FALL
Rating: 3

Fall fish are on the move and coming up to shallower, cooler water. Only when crappie are not yet into the shallows are the deep flats a possible structure. There are exceptions to everything, so keep an open mind when fish aren't present where they should be.

FACTORS
Deep Flats

*Front -normally not too bad.
*Sun/Clouds/Rain -fish may move to a different depth.
*Fast Rise -fish will suspend up or go to shallower water.

Chapter 18

Humps

Humps have been an often ignored structure to many fishermen. However, the increased knowledge of today's fisherman combined with good electronics have made these locations important fishing spots.

Which humps are good? Almost all humps are potential fish factories. Associated depths, slopes, bottom composition, presence of cover and surrounding structures are all important factors in a hump's success.

Why fish humps? Because everything can be present including the above mentioned features. Humps are excellent feeding grounds with fish moving up and down freely, with changes in light penetration, barometric changes and temperatures. Fish numbers can be great around a hump.

Locating a hump is best accomplished with a locator and contour map. Find spots on a map and pinpoint them with a locator. A notebook is a necessity to record landmarks to find the hump again.

Hump

The hump (located just left of center) is a potentially good spot to find fish.
- There's a contour change.
- It's postioned near deep water.
- It should provide a current and/or wave break.
- Depth range to provide a comfort zone.
- Wood cover.

SPRING
Rating: 10

A hump is good in pre-spawn; fish are actively moving. A hump provides protection and possibly good bottom content to promote spawning. Many deep water slabs use humps in the middle of a lake or creek and are never bothered by fishermen.

Post-spawn is another good period for humps because fish go into a general holding pattern for about a week. They still enjoy having depths and cover nearby.

Target humps that are relatively close to other spawning sites. Check for shallow fish with a jig and cork rig. Make long casts and work the jig across all potential areas.

When fish are at the mid depths, spider rig, vertical jig or cast to good drops and cover. Concentrate on the downcurrent side. Insure all types of covers are tested. Spring fishing a hump while others are banging the shoreline can give you a definite edge on catching good quality and numbers. Don't forget to try a few humps when you pattern spring crappie.

SUMMER/WINTER
Rating: 9

Humps that include deep water are top picks for summer or winter crappie. Again, the advantage is many different depths from which a crappie can choose to fit the water conditions. The best humps are good feeding areas, too.

Searches should begin by looking at mid depth and deep areas. A hump with good structure and drop-offs in these depths are sure to hold some fish. Depths can be searched to find the proper range for crappie on a particular day.

Techniques include spider rigging, slow trolling, vertical jigging, and slip-float minnow rigs from an anchored boat. Select your favorite tactic and give it a try.

FALL
Rating: 6

Fall is a hit and miss situation at a hump because crappie are often on the move. However, many humps have everything a fish needs and will hold many crappie while drawing others to the location.

Fall crappie may be at any depth from 2 feet down to 25. Start at 10-12 feet and work up or down from that depth.

FACTORS
Humps

*****Wind** -can be a real problem for fishermen because the humps are often in open water.
*****Strong Front/Clouds/Sun/Rise/Fall** -the beauty of a hump is that fish can slide up or down with temperature, barometric, and light penetration changes to find their best comfort zone.

MORE ON HUMPS
Subject Expert: Jim Perry

Perry & McCadams won the 1996 Crappiethon Classic championship. Team member Jim Perry guides on Kentucky Lake and enjoys fishing humps. He shares a variety of fishing information to help give us an edge when we fish humps.

I have one particular hump that's relatively small. It's about 40 yards either way. I fish it a lot and I'm not the only person who knows about it.

It has stumps. At the bottom of it where it levels off is about 25 feet deep. There are stumps down there at the bottom, at the top and on the slopes.

It has a sharp drop, not a gradual slope. There's mud in the extreme bottom because of the siltation. The sides and top have a relatively hard bottom. This particular one has a lot of clay base with a little gravel mixed in.

How do you locate a hump like this one?

You need a topo map like a US geological map. Original maps before the lake was flooded shows roads and humps.

The particular hump I'm talking about has a river channel running by it. So when I run a depth finder up to it, I come up on the side where the old channel is and the water will drop off to 35 feet. Then it will go up to the 25 foot area, and then up the side. It's got everything.

How do you fish it?

Most of the structure on this hump is on the side where the river channel cuts into it. However, the downcurrent side is good when current is flowing. When current is being pulled, I check the downstream side on any structure. Fish get behind something to get out of the current.

Seasonal Structure 172

Jim Perry pulls a crappie from Kentucky Lake. He recommends that every fisherman should spend time searching for new places. It's interesting, adds versatility to your pattern potential, and gives you a chance to find a hotspot like an isolated hump.

My technique on the humps is the same as on any type of contour. I use a Kentucky Lake minnow rig and run up and down the depth scale. If it's in the winter, they'll be 20 or 25 feet deep. As the water warms they'll just move up that scale.

The depthfinder is usually a good way to find where the fish are located and if they're suspended. If using multiple poles, I can fish different depths and find the fish if they're suspended. Minnows and jigs both work. I just throw it all at 'em and let them tell me.

In the spring it's a little complicated because of different lake elevations. However, they'll be cover-related. One tip is to look on top of a flat. I catch fish on top of that flat even when water is 10 feet deep. They're spawning in open water.

How about summer crappie on your hump?

They just fall off of the hump down the ledge. Again, I play that musical depth scale to find their depth. I can't always predict their depth.

Perry's equipment includes graphite B&M long poles used in pole holders. He likes 6.5 or 7 foot spinning rods for casting.

He uses spinning reels because he can set the drag where he can pull out line by hand to get a foot or two deeper. It's an easy way to judge distance.

Perry's line is Berkley Trilene 8 pound test; sometimes 6. He will sacrifice a few jigs with lighter line to catch more fish.

Chapter 19

High Water Structure

Heavy rains cause many waterways to rise during the spring. The rise can be a few feet to 30 or 40 feet in some Corp of Engineer lakes.

Knowing when and where to catch crappie will be determined by the season and amount of rise. For example, a 5 foot rise may have the best cover in 3-15 feet. If it rises 20 feet, fishing will probably be in 1-10 feet, but some fish may be suspended at these depths over deeper water. Therefore, everything is relative to conditions and the season.

Why fish the high water structures? Because there are very few successful options when water gets too high.

Locating the right structure will be the key to catching fish. Structure may be brush in 3 feet of water or stumps in 25 feet. It may be a road underwater or a culvert with water rushing through. The lake, cover and conditions will dictate the best structure. A fisherman's job is to find the pieces of the puzzle as quickly as possible.

Seasonal Structure 176

SPRING
Rating: 6

Spring gets a low rating for overall fishing but it's great for the situation. All fishing is worse when lake conditions are less than desirable, so this is the best high water rating.

A rise of 5 feet gives you three primary areas to check for fish. The first is very shallow water. Look for crappie way back up in the green brush in 2-3 feet. The green brush filters dirty water and gives protection, so fish hold tight in this cover.

The second place is 5 feet. This is the old shoreline. It's a good spot for fish to associate with the rocks and brush of the old shoreline.

The third place is to look where they were before the rise. Fish in 8 feet before the rise will now be in 13 feet. These fish will stay with the same cover.

Use long pole tactics in the brush. The terribly thick cover calls for an 8-10 foot graphite jig pole. The shorter pole is needed because of all the exposed brush and overhanging limbs. The graphite is needed to detect light strikes.

Jigs are the easiest bait to use in thick cover. Use a 1/16 ounce jig. A tube is standard, but this can be a good time to try specialty jigs. These include a small Match-the-Hatch McKala and the Grizzly jig or a Jaker head Road Runner with a Turbo Tail. Colors should include yellow, red, brown and orange in stained or muddy waters.

Water 10-15 feet high offers more structures for the fish. Look for crappie to move into the cover. They may even stop on the old shoreline. They can be where they were before the rains, but chances are slim they stay that deep.

Techniques are the same as previously discussed. If you prefer to use a minnow, a heavy weight near the hook will allow you to get the minnow in cover with less hanging.

Another tactic is to cast or slow troll along the old shoreline. The type and amount of cover will determine which technique to use.

When water gets 20 or 30 feet high, all bets are off. Fish can go anywhere they want. The amount of extra water scatters them so odds go down tremendously. Finding fish is difficult. They may be in 1 foot or 40 feet. Forming a pattern isn't easy.

The first place to check is the old shoreline where standing timber is located. The fish are likely to be suspended in the tops of the trees. For example, they will be at 12 feet suspended over 25 feet of water.

SUMMER
Rating: 4

Summer high water is different than in the spring because summer fish are located in deeper water. The most common summer high water is due to spring high water that's not been drained. Therefore, the water is falling but is somewhat clear.

A 5 foot high situation has two major tactics to consider. The best choice of fishing is in areas where they would normally be without high water. For example, they will now be at 23 feet if they were at 18 before the rise. It's not uncommon for them to suspend off bottom when the bottom depth is a little deeper than they prefer.

Another pattern is shallower water. Actually, they will move into 12-18 feet on different cover. This isn't shallow, but is usually not as deep as their normal summer depths. Typical cover is logs, stumps and brush piles.

Will crappie go to the shallow brush in the summer? Sure. They will move into the shallows if the temperatures are

High Water Structure

Spring high water quickly sends crappie expert Ed Stewart to the shallow brush. He uses waders to sneak into places a boat cannot go.

moderate and other water is bad. Fish will be scattered.

Water 10, 20 or 30 feet will cause crappie to move up into their comfort zone. For example, 15 feet high water will cause fish to move up. The amount will be determined by the rate of falling water, water conditions and cover available. They may be at the old shoreline in 15 feet of water or out in 20-22 feet on some type of structure.

Almost any mid depth or deep water tactic still work, but I recommend vertical jigging with minnows. This tightlining tactic targets specific structure where fish should be located. Tightlining gives good bait control and lets all of the depths and cover be fished as fast or slow as you want.

OUTLINE OF A HEAVY RAIN

(1) Day prior to rain. Fish are active; good fishing.

(2) Day of rain. Fish are in very shallow or they move out to deeper 'sweet' water not yet muddy with a bad pH.

(3) Day two. Fish are in the clearest water locations. Deep into the shallow brush is a likely warm weather position. They will be very scattered.

(4) Day three-four. Fish back to their typical locations if rise is not too high.

(5) Day five to thirty. On a large rise, fish will gradually move back to original locations as the water recedes.

FALL
Rating: 4

Fall is less likely to have high water. However, when the waters rise, conditions change. The fish may move but some will stay and bite. Stumps, logs, islands and wake walls are good fall high water structures.

A small rise will not move crappie. A larger rise will force them to move. Current may be a major factor in the fall. Look for fish to move to shallow water. Simply match the baits and tactics to the conditions and structures.

WINTER
Rating: 4

This is not the season for a lot of high water. It could happen, but it's normally not the time for major rains. Also, it's the time when many lakes are brought down to a low water level to prepare for spring rains.

High water winter crappie prefer to stay on cover they've selected for the winter. Since many of these places are along the river and creek channels, current will be a problem and may drive them elsewhere. The rise and current will dictate their movements.

Tactics are the same as any other season in high water. The targets in winter are typically stumps. They provide good deep cover and protect the fish from moderate currents.

TIP -Mud is often a problem when dealing with high water. Check different areas for different water colors; test each type by fishing. Also stay away from bad current.

Seasonal Structure   182

Roy Saddler working high water brush.

Small, man-made boat designed for shallow water and places where a larger boat can't get.

Products Mentioned

AWD Baits 803-438-2110	Crappie Firetail Delights
B&M 800-647-6363	Jigging Poles
Bass Pro Shops 800-BASS-PRO	Wally Marshall Poles
Berkley 800-237-5539	Trilene; Fireline
Blakemore 417-334-5340	Road Runner; Jaker head; Turbo Tail
Blue Fox 612-689-3402	Crappie Spin
Cabela's 800-237-4444	Marabou
Crappie Company USA 573-624-2208	Umbrella tubes
Crappie USA 615-377-7800	National Tournament Trail
Crappie World 1-800-554-1999	Magazine
Grizzly Jig Company 800-305-9866	Google-Eye jig; Grizzly jig
Jadico/ Laker 314-346-4305	Curly Bug; Paddle Bug
JWA Johnson 800-299-2592	Beetle Spin
Lake Systems 800-641-4371	Combo-C-Lector
(Bill) Lewis Lures 318-487-0352	Tiny Trap; Rattle Trap
McKala Fishing, LLC 800-307-7064	Match-the-Hatch jigs
Storm Lures 405-329-5894	PeeWee Wart
Zebco/Quantum 918-836-5581	Crappie-Finder reel; Rods

Guides/ Professionals

Roger Gant 601-287-2017	Pickwick crappie guide
Wally Marshall 214-272-4016	Pro Crappie Advisor
Guy Winters 314-346-4305	Fisherman; seminar speaker
Norm Trautman 816-438-7574	Truman Lake guide
Sam Heaton 800-791-3798	Weiss Lake guide; JWA promotions
Tim & Chatt Martin 913-764-5746	Fishing team; seminar speakers
Steve McCadams 901-642-0360	Kentucky Lake (Tenn) guide
Jim Perry 901-642-8870	Kentucky Lake (Tenn) guide
Darrell Van Vactor 502-395-4204	Crappie USA president

Special Thanks

To everyone who contributed information, interviews and assistance for completion of this book.

To Pam Credille for proof reading.

To the Corps of Engineers for providing use of portions of topo maps for illustrations.

Seasonal Structure 188

Contour maps are being studied by fishermen the day before a tournament. Selecting potential areas and spot-checking for quality fish is an efficient method of finding the best holes.

Huffman Publishing
Outdoor Education & Entertainment

Winning Crappie Secrets
Book featuring the best crappie fishing team in the country: Ronnie Capps and Steve Coleman, the '95 and '97 Classic Champs. Topics include: Slow vertical trolling; key spots to fish; equipment and rigging; bait rigs; pro pointers; over 45 photographs and drawings. Released December 1996.

Wappapello Sportsman's Guide
Light, interesting reading about the Wappapello Lake area. About half of the book is devoted to catching all the different species of fish on the lake. Also included: hunting; camping; hiking; and more. 128 pages. Released December 1997.

You may order by sending check or money order to:

Huffman Publishing
PO Box 26
Poplar Bluff, MO 63902

Prices include: s&h plus any applicable tax

Winning Crappie Secrets $10.50
Wappapello Sportsman's Guide $8.00
Seasonal Structures for Crappie $11.50

Seasonal Structure 192

SLABS
What a way to end a crappie fishing book..... looking at a couple huge slabs. These fish were taken from Kentucky Lake by the man with a big smile, Jim Carman.